Take &Read

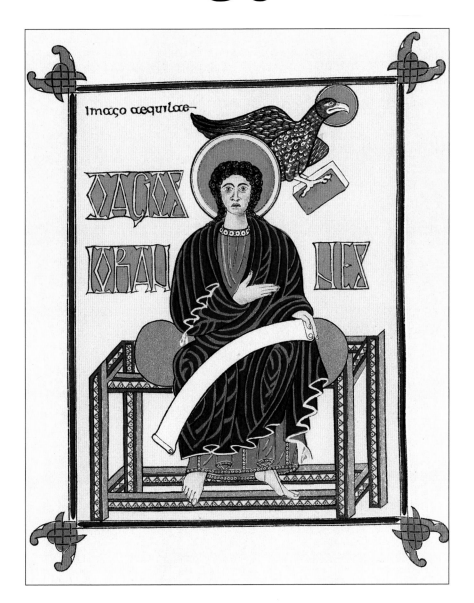

Imago aequilae

The Gospel of John

John J. Henry,
Edited by Adrian Graffy

First published in 2009 by Alive Publishing Ltd.

Graphic House, 124 City Road, Stoke on Trent, ST4 2PH.

Tel: +44 (0) 1782 745600   Fax: +44 (0) 1782 745500

www.alivepublishing.co.uk

©2009 Alive Publishing

British Library Catalogue-in-Publication Data.

A catalogue record for this book is available from the British Library.

ISBN 978-1-906278-07-6

Cover image and previous page: St. John with his symbol, from the Lindisfarne Gospels, 710-721, English School, (8th century).

Contents

Page 5   Foreword

Page 7   Introduction to the Gospel of John

Page 9   The Witness of John the Baptist

Page 22   The Coming of the First Disciples to Jesus

Page 36   The Wedding at Cana in Galilee

Page 48   Jesus and Nicodemus

Page 62   Jesus and the Samaritan Woman

Page 74   The Feeding of the Five Thousand

Page 86   The Discourse on the Bread of Life

Page 98   Jesus as Sheepgate and Shepherd

Page 110   The Arrest of Jesus

Page 122   The Death of Jesus

Page 134   The Appearances of Jesus to the Disciples

Page 148   The Prologue

Page 162   Picture credits

Foreword

One of the features of the Church of today is the rediscovery of the Bible. In the years since the Second Vatican Council this thirst for the Scriptures has become stronger and stronger. The desire for a deeper engagement with the Bible is clear from the enormous popularity of publications such as *Walk with Me* and *Bible Alive*.

Take and Read is designed to assist people in their need to understand the Bible more deeply. The series has been developed as a follow-up to the document *'The Gift of Scripture'*, which was produced in 2005 by the Bishops of England and Wales, and of Scotland, to mark the 40th anniversary of the Council document on Divine Revelation, *Dei Verbum*.

The story of the conversion of Saint Augustine to the Catholic faith inspired the title of the series. He recounts in his 'Confessions' how he heard a voice calling to him with the words *Tolle, lege* 'Take and Read'. At that moment he picked up the New Testament and read the first chapter his eyes fell upon, from the Letter to the Romans. His conversion was assured.

These books are a major new resource for prayerful reading of the Scriptures both for groups and for individuals. Passages from the Gospels are accompanied by commentary, quotations from the Fathers and from Church documents, Christian art and inspiring photographs, as well as suggestions for prayer and reflection.

It is a great pleasure to acknowledge the work of those who helped develop this series. Representatives from dioceses throughout Britain worked on the preparatory stages. Particular thanks should go to Anne White, Anne Dixon and Sister Vicky Hummell. I record my gratitude to the authors who have produced such rich commentary on the gospel passages. I am particularly pleased that Mike and Sue Conway of Alive Publishing agreed to publish the *Take and Read* series.

Take and Read will help you to delve more deeply into the Scriptures, to understand them better, and to pray with the Scriptures. *Take and Read* will assist you in *lectio divina*, that prayerful reading of Scripture which has always been central to the life of the Church.

Fr Adrian Graffy

And behold I heard a voice from a nearby house singing and frequently repeating, like a boy or a girl, I do not know which: Take and read; take and read. I grabbed the book and opened it and I read in silence the first chapter my eyes fell upon.

Augustine Confessions VIII, 29

I pray you, good Jesus,
that as you have graciously granted me to take
in with delight
the words that give knowledge of you,
so you will grant me in your kindness
to come at last to you, the source of all wisdom,
and to stand for ever before your face. Amen.

The Prayer of St Bede (to end a session)

Introduction to the Gospel of John

The Gospel of John is unique among the four gospels. It shares only a couple of miracle stories with the first three gospels. Its healing miracles are quite different, and it has no exorcisms of people who were possessed. Instead of just one journey of Jesus to Jerusalem, it has various visits by him during his ministry, as well as a short stay in Samaria.

In addition, the teaching given by Jesus is remarkably different. Instead of the practical, agricultural or everyday parables of the first three gospels, the teaching in John's gospel is at a much higher, sublime and solemn level, coming across as God's word of revelation for humanity, with Jesus as God's revealer. This gospel contains memorable discourses by Jesus on themes such as rebirth, water, food, harvest, bread of life, judgment, light, blindness, sheep, shepherd and sheepgate, as well as three chapters of farewell discourse (14-16), and one of prayer by Jesus (17). It is small wonder that this gospel has been prized by many since early times as a valued source of spiritual nourishment.

Since the time of St Irenaeus (around 200 AD) this gospel has been linked with John the Apostle, taken to be 'the disciple whom Jesus loved'. Even if, as some maintain, St John did not himself physically write it, he may well have been the source and authority behind much that went into the gospel when it was written down late in the first century AD.

In this book you will find twelve sessions, each presenting a section of the gospel for study and prayer. These twelve sections will give you a good idea of John's gospel and help you to understand it more deeply, but it will help you further if you use your own Bible to read the intervening sections of the gospel that are not in this book.

Opposite: St. John the Baptist, 1513-16 by Leonardo da Vinci, (1452-1519).

The Witness of John the Baptist

Hear the Word of God

Read John 1:19-34

19 This is the testimony given by John when the Jews sent priests and Levites from Jerusalem to ask him, 'Who are you?' 20 He confessed and did not deny it, but confessed, 'I am not the Messiah.' 21 And they asked him, 'What then? Are you Elijah?' He said, 'I am not.' 'Are you the prophet?' He answered, 'No.'

22 Then they said to him, 'Who are you? Let us have an answer for those who sent us. What do you say about yourself?'

23 He said, 'I am the voice of one crying out in the wilderness, 'Make straight the way of the Lord,' ' as the prophet Isaiah said.

24 Now they had been sent from the Pharisees.

25 They asked him, 'Why then are you baptising if you are neither the Messiah, nor Elijah, nor the prophet?'

26 John answered them, 'I baptise with water. Among you stands one whom you do not know, 27 the one who is coming after me; I am not worthy to untie the thong of his sandal.'

28 This took place in Bethany across the Jordan, where John was baptising.

29 The next day he saw Jesus coming towards him and declared, 'Here is the Lamb of God who takes away the sin of the world! 30 This is he of whom I said, 'After me comes a man who ranks ahead of me, because he was before me.' 31 I myself did not know him; but I came baptising with water for this reason, that he might be revealed to Israel.'

32 And John testified, 'I saw the spirit descending from heaven like a dove, and it remained on him. 33 I myself did not know him, but the one who sent me to baptise with water said to me, 'He on whom you see the Spirit descend and remain is the one who baptises with the Holy Spirit.' 34 And I myself have seen and have testified that this is the Son of God.'

Understand the Word of God

This session will explore:

- ❖ the testimony of John the Baptist about his own role
- ❖ his testimony about Jesus
- ❖ the description of Jesus as 'the Lamb of God'

Setting in the Gospel

This is the first narrative section of the Fourth Gospel. It is preceded by the Prologue *(John* 1:1-18), a hymn of the Johannine church to Christ as the 'Word' or 'Logos'. This hymn may have been inserted as the opening of the gospel at a later stage of the editing of the gospel. The Prologue, with its focus on Christ as God's eternal Word, is a magnificent and inspiring introduction to this gospel, and also a good summary of it. We shall look at the Prologue as the last of our passages.

The Bodmer P75 manuscript (left) shows the beginning of John's Gospel. It dates to about 200AD and was recently donated to the Vatican Library.

What Kind of Text?

This passage concerns John the Baptist's testimony to his own role, in verses 19-28, and then, in verses 29-34, his witness to Jesus, who appeared on the scene. 'Witness' or 'testimony' is the important word associated with John the Baptist in the Fourth Gospel. He is, in this gospel, quite simply a witness to Jesus, having no significance apart from him. John 'testifies' to Jesus. He is not depicted as preaching a baptism of repentance, as he is in the synoptic gospels. Jesus, by contrast, does not speak at all.

John 1:7 He came as a witness to testify to the light

John 1:19 This is the testimony given by John.

John 1:32 And John testified

Mark 1:4 John the baptiser appeared in the wilderness, proclaiming a baptism of repentance for the forgiveness of sins.

John the Baptist depicted in stained glass in a modern Catholic Church.

Commentary: verse by verse reading

The Words of John the Baptist about Himself

v.19 This could have been the start of the Fourth Gospel, before the Prologue, or 'Hymn to the Logos', was added to provide the Gospel with such a suitable opening hymn of praise, at a late stage of editing.

'Testimony' can also be translated 'witness'. It is an important Johannine word, and occurs some fourteen times in the gospel. 'Witness' is an indispensable idea in John's notion of faith, in that the nature and dignity of the incarnate Word have to be made known to the readers of the gospel through the testimony of others. 'Witness' or 'testimony' (Greek *marturia*) is therefore primarily religious in meaning in the Fourth Gospel, although at times, as here, when it occurs in an official 'interrogation', it can also have a juridical meaning. The Greek word gives us the English 'martyr', one who gives up his or her life in witness.

The term 'the Jews' occurs frequently in John, more than seventy times. Very often, but not always, it is used in a hostile sense. The Levites were an inferior priestly class. They provided police and some menial services for the Temple. They are only rarely mentioned in the New Testament, as in the Parable of the Good Samaritan (*Luke* 19:32). Barnabas in Acts 4:36 is said to have been a Levite.

v.20 The language in this verse is repetitious: 'he confessed .... he did not deny .... he confessed'. 'I am not the Messiah' is presumably meant here in the exact sense: 'I am not the expected anointed Davidic king.'

In the synoptic gospels John the Baptist asks the question about Jesus, 'Are you the one who is to come, or are we to wait for another?' (*Matthew* 11:3 *Luke* 7:19). In the Fourth Gospel, the Baptist regards Jesus from the outset as the Messiah, and he is quite clear that he, the Baptist, is not the Messiah.

The Pontifical Biblical Commission gives the following teaching about the use of the term 'the Jews' in the Gospel of John:

It has been noted with good reason that much of the Fourth Gospel anticipates the trial of Jesus and gives him the opportunity to defend himself and accuse his accusers. These are often called 'the Jews' without further precision, with the result that an unfavourable judgement is associated with that name. But there is no question here of anti-Jewish sentiment, since the Gospel recognises that 'salvation comes from the Jews' (4:22). This manner of speaking only reflects the clear separation that existed between the Christian and Jewish communities. (The Jewish People and their Sacred Scriptures in the Christian Bible 76)

v.21 John the Baptist now denies that he is Elijah the prophet. According to Mark (9:13) and Matthew (11:14), Jesus identified John the Baptist as the Elijah who was to return: 'I tell you that he has come....'. The Jewish expectation was that Elijah would have to return before the Messiah came. According to that thinking (which is not in mind in the Fourth Gospel), if Elijah had not done so, Jesus could not be the Messiah.

The Book of Malachi tells us of the expected return of Elijah:

Lo, I will send you the prophet Elijah before the great and terrible day of the Lord comes. He will turn the hearts of parents to their children and the hearts of children to their parents, so that I will not come and strike the land with a curse.

(Malachi 4:5-6 / 3:23-24)

Elijah in the Desert, 1818 by Washington Allston, (1779-1843).

John the Baptist denies he is 'the prophet'. This is probably a reference to the prophet like Moses in Deuteronomy 18:15: 'The Lord your God will raise up for you a prophet like me from among your own people; you shall heed such a prophet.'

vv.22-23 The quote applied to the work of John the Baptist in verse 23 is from Isaiah 40:3. While in the synoptic gospels it is stated by the gospel-writers, here it is spoken by John himself, and given in an abbreviated form. Instead of 'prepare the way of the Lord, make straight his paths' (*Mark* 1:3), here we have 'make straight the way of the Lord.'

It is notable how humble the Baptist's claims for himself are. His is an unknown, unidentified, anonymous voice.

v.24 That they were 'sent from the Pharisees' is unlikely. Most of the priests and Levites would have been Sadducees, not Pharisees. It was only after 70 AD and the destruction of Jerusalem that Judaism became predominantly Pharisaic. Probably this misinformation reflects the situation in the author's day, rather than in Jesus' day.

vv.25-26 Unlike his audience, John the Baptist does know, and has already recognised, the one who is coming, through the revelation given to him. He does not name the one he is talking about. The people are not just ignorant for the moment, but deeply estranged, lacking any readiness to accept the one who is to come.

The idea of the 'unknown Messiah' will be mentioned at 7:27: 'when the Messiah comes, no one will know where he is from'.

v.27 The Baptist's words about not being worthy to untie the thong of Jesus' sandal remind us of the similar statement in Mark 1:7-8: 'the one who is more powerful than I is coming after me; I am not worthy to stoop down and untie the thong of his sandals.' But the Fourth Evangelist has not taken the words from Mark; the words in the Greek originals are different.

v.28 The site of this 'Bethany across the Jordan' is unknown. It is not the Bethany two miles from Jerusalem, where, according to 11:18, Martha, Mary and Lazarus lived. This 'Bethany across the Jordan' will be implied, though not named, later, at 10:40, when Jesus goes back there, apparently to withdraw from people, towards the close of his ministry. John 10:40 reads: 'He went away again across the Jordan to the place where John had been baptising earlier, and he remained there.'

The departure of the envoys from John the Baptist is not narrated. There is often a narrative incompleteness in the Fourth Gospel, and in verse 29 it is not clear whom the Baptist is addressing. Details that the modern reader might expect are not important for the evangelist, whose interest is in the theological, rather than the historical.

In Jesus' day the religious scene among the Jews was dominated by Sadducees and Pharisees.

The Sadducees were the more powerful and mostly priestly group, who tended to collaborate with the Roman occupation. The Pharisees were closer to the common people. By the time this gospel was written, after the destruction of Jerusalem in 70 AD, the Sadducees were no longer a force to be reckoned with, and 'Pharisaism' had much greater importance.

St John Chrysostom, the great biblical scholar and preacher, who was bishop of Constantinople in the 4th century, comments on the Baptist's outspokenness:

He was not in a house, not in a corner, not in the wilderness, but in the middle of the multitude. This was after he had made his presence known at the Jordan when all that were baptised by him were present. It was here that he proclaimed aloud that wonderful confession concerning Christ, full of those sublime and great and mysterious doctrines. It was here that he said he was not worthy to unloose the strap of his shoe.

(Homilies on the Gospel of John 17.1)

The Lamb of God

The sequence of seven days can be tracked down in the following verses:

1:19 (the first day)

1:29 the next day

1:35 the next day

1:43 the next day

2:1 On the third day

The Catechism of the Catholic Church reads:

John the Baptist looked at Jesus and pointed him out as the 'Lamb of God, who takes away the sin of the world'. By doing so, he reveals that Jesus is at the same time the suffering Servant who silently allows himself to be led to the slaughter and who bears the sin of the multitudes, and also the Paschal Lamb, the symbol of Israel's redemption at the first Passover. (608)

The words of John the Baptist are taken up in the words of the priest at Mass:

Behold the Lamb of God, who takes away the sins of the world.

They are also found in the Agnus Dei (Lamb of God) before Holy Communion.

v.29 There appears to be a sequence of seven days in the section that goes from John 1:19 to 2:1. It has long been suggested that an inaugural week of the ministry of Jesus is being deliberately presented, hinting at the idea of a new creation in Jesus, just as the first creation was accomplished in one week, according to Genesis 1.

The title 'Lamb of God' occurs again in the Gospel of John at John 1:36. There are various ways of understanding the phrase. 'The Lamb' is a symbol of Christ frequently mentioned in the Book of Revelation as the one who would destroy evil at the end of time (*Revelation* 5:9 and 17:14). Alternatively, the Servant of the Lord in the Book of Isaiah is described metaphorically as going like a sheep to his slaughter, like a lamb dumb before his shearers (*Isaiah* 53:7). There may also be an allusion to the killing of the paschal lamb, which ensured the protection of the Jews about to leave Egypt (*Exodus* 12). Possibly the usage here of 'Lamb of God' combines the two ideas of the paschal lamb and the Servant of the Lord.

The Lamb of God 'takes away the sin of the world'. The present tense appears to have a future force, 'will take away'. This is more than just 'bearing', or taking on oneself the sin of others and the punishment due for it. It is taking it away completely. 'The sin of the world' refers to the sinful state of the world, which is of course the sum of the sinful acts of many individuals. St Paul uses a variety of plural nouns for 'sin', such as 'transgressions', but the Fourth Evangelist prefers to use the collective singular noun, 'sin'.

Could John the Baptist have spoken at this time and in this way of the future death of Jesus? Or is this the theology of the evangelist and his community, placed on the lips of John the Baptist? John will again refer to Jesus as 'Lamb of God' in verse 36.

v.30 The comparison between Jesus and John is in terms of time and rank: 'after me.. ..ranks ahead of me.. ..was before me.' 'After me' means following in time, not following after, as a disciple. 'He was before me' appears to be an affirmation of the pre-existence of Jesus, and therefore quite an advanced understanding of Jesus on the part of John the Baptist. This may again be the theology of the evangelist and his community, which has been placed on the lips of the Baptist. Perhaps the Baptist's testimony to Jesus' superiority led immediately in the evangelist's mind to the thought of Jesus' pre-existence.

v.31 The idea of the hidden Messiah seems to be presupposed here: that the Messiah would be unknown and hidden, until the day he was made known to the people. 'I myself did not know him' contradicts Luke's gospel, according to which the mothers of Jesus and John the Baptist knew one another, as kinswomen. Furthermore, Elizabeth says to Mary in Luke 1:44: 'As soon as I heard the sound of your greeting, the child in my womb leaped for joy.'

Witnessing to Jesus is the whole purpose both of John's ministry and of his baptising according to the Fourth Gospel. 'Israel' here refers to the circle around John the Baptist. 'Israel' occurs only four times in John, and has good, positive connotations, unlike 'the Jews', which so often has negative connotations in this gospel.

This gospel has no narrative of Jesus being baptised by John the Baptist. The evangelist does not portray John the Baptist as celebrating a baptism of repentance for the forgiveness of sin, precisely because it is the Lamb who takes away the sin of the world. The absence of a baptism narrative may also connect with the problem of the continuing existence in the evangelist's day of followers of John the Baptist, who venerated the Baptist, but not Jesus. An account of Jesus being baptised by John might be misused to suggest that Jesus was inferior to John.

v.32 These words remind us of the baptism of Jesus in the other gospels. Though he does not narrate the story, the evangelist appears to know about it. In Mark and Matthew it is Jesus who sees the Spirit descending after his baptism by John. Here the Baptist says that he saw the Spirit come down on Jesus like a dove.

'Remain' (Greek *menein*) is an important Johannine word. It is also translated 'stay' or 'abide'. Here it is about the permanence of Jesus' possession of the Spirit, which 'remained' on him.

v.33 'I did not know him' repeats verse 31. 'The one who sent me' is more often in the gospel a reference to the Father sending Jesus. Here it is used by John the Baptist about his own mission.

In the synoptic gospels, God's testimony to Jesus is given by the voice from heaven after the baptism (*Mark* 1:11). Here it is given, not in a voice from heaven, but, at second hand, through John the Baptist, who speaks of what he saw and heard. The Baptist claims to have both seen the descent of the dove, and to have heard God speak to him.

The one who will baptise with the Spirit is the coming Messiah. Quite how the Baptist understood this 'baptising with the Holy Spirit' we are not told. The same distinction between baptism in water and in the Holy Spirit is also found in the other gospels (*Matthew* 3:11 *Luke* 3:16). Such a distinction, between water and spirit, was unknown in the prophecies of the Old Testament. Ezekiel 36:25-26 reads: 'I will sprinkle clean water upon you, and you shall be clean from all your uncleanness and all your idols ... a new heart I will give you, and a new spirit I will put within you.'

Do we understand this as 'baptises with the Holy Spirit', or 'with holy spirit'? There is no definite article in the Greek, and the ancient manuscripts did not make a lower-case / upper-case distinction. As said by John the Baptist, it would not have been a distinct person of the Trinity that was spoken of. 'Spirit' could have been regarded as a divine property or attribute. On the other hand, as elsewhere, words attributed to the Baptist may have had a much fuller meaning for the evangelist and his community.

v.34 'This is the Son of God' is the reading of the majority of ancient manuscripts, but a few read 'the Chosen One' or 'the Elect of God'. This would be a reference to Isaiah 42:1: 'my servant whom I uphold, my chosen one in whom my soul delights'. If 'Son of God' is the correct reading, it would probably have been meant by the Baptist in a messianic sense, though the evangelist would be hinting at a fuller idea of 'Son'.

Since there is no baptism story, John 1:19-35 narrates, surprisingly, the only personal contact between Jesus and the Baptist in this gospel, and the Baptist is the only one to speak.

St Augustine of Hippo, one of the greatest fathers of the Latin Church, who lived from 354-430, comments:

It was appropriate then that the Holy Spirit should be manifested in this way descending on our Lord so that everyone who had the Spirit might know that he ought to be simple as a dove and be in sincere peace with his brothers and sisters.

(Tractates on the Gospel of John 6)

Titles and Descriptions of Jesus in John 1:19-34

v.26 one whom you do not know

v.29 the Lamb of God who takes away the sin of the world

v.30 the one who ranks ahead of John the Baptist, because he was before him

v.33 the one on whom the Spirit descended and remained ... who baptises with the Holy Spirit

v.34 the Son of God.

The Word Lives On

We have observed how the words of John the Baptist have been taken up into the liturgy of the Eucharist. The chant of the *Agnus Dei* was in fact introduced into the Mass by Pope Sergius (687-701). It was one of the last things to be added to the Mass. The text of the *Agnus Dei* has been set to music hundreds of times, whether in Latin chant or in the compositions of major composers, or recent more modern settings. It is curious that while the text of John's gospel has John the Baptist refer to Jesus taking away 'the sin' of the world, the liturgical text of the *Agnus Dei* has 'the sins' of the world, and the words of the priest which follow are: 'Behold the Lamb of God who takes away the sins of the world!'

In the Lectionary

The section on the witness of John the Baptist (*John* 1:19-28) is the gospel reading for the 3rd Sunday of Advent in Year B. The same text is read during the Christmas Season on 2nd January.

The section on John's witness to Jesus (*John* 1:29-34) is the gospel reading for the 2nd Sunday in Ordinary Time in Year A. The text is also read during the Christmas Season on 3rd January.

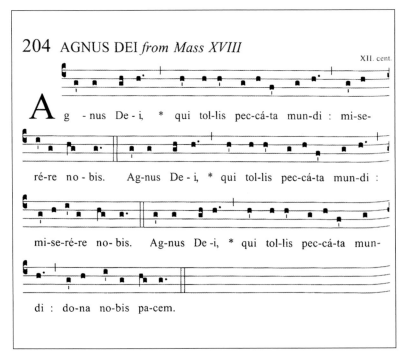

204 AGNUS DEI *from Mass XVIII*

XII. cent.

A g - nus De - i, * qui tol-lis pec-cá-ta mun-di : mi-se-ré-re no - bis. Ag-nus De - i, * qui tol-lis pec-cá-ta mun-di : mi-se-ré-re no- bis. Ag-nus De -i, * qui tol-lis pec-cá-ta mun-di : do-na no-bis pa-cem.

From The Adoremus Hymnal, produced by Adoremus: Society for the Renewal of the Sacred Liturgy © 1997, Ignatius Press, San Francisco. Used with permission.

Live the Word of God

Listen once more to the reading

What do you hear now?
Suggestions for reflection and prayer

What is the mission of John the Baptist according to John's gospel?

Reflect on the text from St Bede given in the margin.

Why does the Fourth Gospel avoid detailed reference to the baptism of Jesus?

John the Baptist is honest about his own role and does not claim more than is his due.

❖ Pray for the grace of discernment of our vocation, and the humility to accept whatever God wills us to do.

John the Baptist bears witness to the truth about Jesus.

❖ Pray for those who bear witness to the truth at the risk of persecution and death.

John the Baptist tells us that the essence of Jesus' ministry is to take away the sin of the world.

❖ Pray for a deeper understanding and acceptance of the saving work of Christ.

The Baptist speaks of the coming baptism of believers in Christ.

❖ Pray for a deeper appreciation of the new life baptism brings.

St Bede, monk of Jarrow in the 7th and 8th centuries and great commentator on the Scriptures, describes how the Lamb, who is Jesus, slays the lion (= Satan):

Jesus gave his blood as the price for our salvation, and by undergoing death for a time he condemned the sovereignty of death forever. The Lamb that was innocent was killed. But by a wonderful and longed-for display of his power he efficaciously weakened the strength of the lion that had killed him. The Lamb that took away the sins of the world brought to naught the lion that had brought sins into the world. It was the Lamb that restored us by the offering of his flesh and blood so that we would not perish. (Homilies on the Gospels 2.7)

St. John the Baptist by Jacopo Palma, (Il Vecchio) (c.1480-1528).

The Coming of the
First Disciples to Jesus

Hear the Word of God

Read John 1:35-51

³⁵ The next day John was again standing with two of his disciples, ³⁶ and, as he watched Jesus walk by, he exclaimed, 'Look, here is the Lamb of God.'

³⁷ The two disciples heard him say this, and they followed Jesus.

³⁸ When Jesus turned and saw them following, he said to them, 'What are you looking for?' They said to him, 'Rabbi' (which translated means Teacher), 'where are you staying?' ³⁹ He said to them, 'Come and see.' They came and saw where he was staying, and they remained with him that day. It was about four o'clock in the afternoon.

⁴⁰ One of the two who heard John speak and followed him was Andrew, Simon Peter's brother. ⁴¹ He first found his brother Simon and said to him, 'We have found the Messiah' (which is translated Anointed). ⁴² He brought Simon to Jesus, who looked at him and said, 'You are Simon son of John. You are to be called Kephas' (which is translated Peter).

⁴³ The next day Jesus decided to go to Galilee. He found Philip and said to him, 'Follow me.' ⁴⁴ Now Philip was from Bethsaida, the city of Andrew and Peter.

⁴⁵ Philip found Nathanael, and said to him, 'We have found him about whom Moses in the law and also the prophets wrote, Jesus son of Joseph from Nazareth.'

⁴⁶ Nathanael said to him, 'Can anything good come out of Nazareth?' Philip said to him, 'Come and see.'

⁴⁷ When Jesus saw Nathanael coming towards him, he said of him, 'Here is truly an Israelite in whom there is no deceit!' ⁴⁸ Nathanael asked him, 'Where did you come to know me?' Jesus answered, 'I saw you under the fig tree before Philip called you.' ⁴⁹ Nathanael replied, 'Rabbi, you are the Son of God! You are the king of Israel!' ⁵⁰ Jesus answered, 'Do you believe because I told you that I saw you under the fig tree? You will see greater things than these.' ⁵¹ And he said to him, 'Very truly, I tell you, you will see heaven opened, and the angels of God ascending and descending upon the Son of Man.'

Opposite: The Calling of the First Four Disciples by Frank Wesley.

Understand the Word of God

This session will explore:

- ❖ the call of the first disciples in the Fourth Gospel
- ❖ their rapid growth in faith
- ❖ the new name given to Simon
- ❖ the dialogue with Nathanael

Setting in the Gospel

The passage follows immediately from the previous one. We noted while examining John 1:19-34 that there was a sequence of days beginning, which continues through chapter 1 and into chapter 2. The sequence began in 1:19 when John the Baptist gave his testimony about himself. 'The next day' (= the second day of the sequence), when John first pointed to Jesus as the 'Lamb of God', comes in 1:29. The third and fourth days appear in our present passage in 1:35 and 1:43. The sequence will be concluded with the phrase 'on the third day' in 2:1, which introduces the story of the Wedding at Cana and completes the week. As our passage begins, John the Baptist is still on the scene, but not for long.

John the Baptist sees Jesus from Afar by James Tissot

- 24 -

What Kind of Text?

This is very different from the calling of the first disciples in the other gospels, where Simon and Andrew are fishing, and James and John are mending nets (*Mark* 1:16-20). In the Fourth Gospel there is no such setting, and no hint that these first disciples are fishermen. The other gospels give no suggestion that the disciples had been followers of John the Baptist, as they are in John's gospel. Furthermore, according to the Fourth Gospel, the ministries of the Baptist and of Jesus overlap to some extent, while, according to Mark 1:14, the ministry of Jesus began only after John's arrest.

The Fourth Gospel also compresses the disciples' growth in their understanding of Jesus. Already in the first chapter of the gospel a remarkable number of titles are bestowed on Jesus by John the Baptist and by the disciples.

Commentary: verse by verse reading
The Call of the First Three Disciples

v.35 This is the third day of the 'inaugural week', and the setting is apparently still Bethany beyond the Jordan (v. 28).

v.36 'Watched' means 'looked with insight and penetration', and the same verb will be used in verse 42 of Jesus looking at Simon. 'Look, here is the Lamb of God' is a shorter version of verse 29, which had 'who takes away the sin of the world'.

After verses 35-36 John the Baptist fades from the scene. He makes only one more appearance in this gospel, beginning at 3:25, in a discussion with his disciples. He gives further testimony to Jesus and declares: 'He (Jesus) must increase, but I must decrease.' (3:30)

v.37 One of the two disciples is identified in verse 40 as Andrew. The other is not identified. He is not Philip, who is found the next day in verse 43. Some suggest that he is the evangelist. He might be, though nothing in the text demands the identification.

The Calling of St. Andrew and St. John, illustration for 'The Life of Christ', c.1886-94. Artist: James Tissot, (1836-1902).

The two disciples 'follow' Jesus. Even if, at this stage, it is not much more than idle curiosity on their part, 'follow' is the term used of the action of disciples, who follow in faith. These two are portrayed as already acting like disciples. It is a literal, physical following of Jesus by them, but it is also their first step to faith. It leads to their 'remaining' with Jesus that day, and, after that, remaining with him permanently.

v.38 'What are you looking for/seeking?' This question is addressed also to the reader of the gospel. Jesus will ask the soldiers who come to arrest him 'whom do you seek?' (18:4), and a similar question is directed to Mary Magdalene, who seeks his body at the empty tomb, and supposes him to be the gardener (20:15).

'Rabbi' is translated by the evangelist for the benefit of the readers. Commonly used of Jewish teachers, it means literally 'my great one'. Its usage may be unhistorical for the ministry of Jesus, since it was probably not used as a title or address for a teacher until late in the first century. It is used as an address eight times in the Fourth Gospel, but only a few times in Matthew and Mark.

v.39 'Coming to' Jesus and 'seeing' are used by the Fourth Gospel to describe belief, the journey of faith. Compare the parallel statement in John 6:35: 'Whoever comes to me will never be hungry, and whoever believes in me will never be thirsty.' See also the statement in John 12:45 about seeing: 'Whoever sees me sees the one who sent me.' 'Come and see' is literally 'Come and you will see.' It is a promise as well as an invitation. Philip will use the same words of invitation and promise to Nathanael in verse 46.

'Where he was staying' and 'they remained' use the same verb in the Greek (*menein*). It is used three times in verses 38- 39, with the deeper theological meaning of 'dwelling', 'abiding'. Jesus will later say to the disciples: 'If you abide (remain, dwell) in me, and my words abide in you, ask for whatever you wish, and it will be done for you.' (*John* 15:7).

'Four o'clock' in the translation is literally 'the tenth hour', day-time being calculated from 6 am. Some commentators think that it might imply the beginning of a sabbath day, with its restrictions on travel. But that is speculation.

The impression given is that these two seekers are won over by Jesus himself, and that John the Baptist was only an intermediary. We are not told where Jesus was staying, for it is unimportant, nor of the contents of their conversation with him. What is important is the person of Jesus - his majesty, his power to win people.

v.40 Simon Peter is here given his two names in their Greek form. In Hebrew he would have been called 'Simeon Kepha'. It seems almost to be taken for granted that the reader knows about these two disciples, Peter and Andrew.

Other instances where Jesus is addressed as 'Rabbi':

John 3:2 Rabbi, we know that you are a teacher who has come from God.

John 4:31 Rabbi, eat something.

John 9:2 Rabbi, who sinned, this man or his parents, that he was born blind?

Mark 9:5 Rabbi, it is good for us to be here.

Mark 14:45 Judas said, 'Rabbi!', and kissed him.

In Orthodox Christianity Andrew is given the title protokletos, 'the first-called'. Orthodox Christians have a profound reverence for Andrew, the brother of Peter, and it has become customary for the Church of Rome to send greetings to the Orthodox Ecumenical Patriarch on 30th November, the feast of St Andrew.

v.41 Andrew 'first' found his brother Simon. 'First' is used in the sense of before doing anything else. It is an unexpected word here, in that no further action of Andrew is recounted. Andrew's activity here, and Philip's later in verse 45, show them to be already acting as disciples. They speak for Jesus, and bring others to him.

'Messiah' is given in its Hebrew form, which the evangelist explains in Greek for his readers, '*Christos*', 'anointed one'. The confession of Jesus as 'the Christ' occurs in the synoptic gospels at Caesarea Philippi, where it is made by Peter, half-way through the gospel (*Mark 8:27-30*). Here it is made early on, and by Andrew.

v.42 Just as John the Baptist looked at Jesus in John 1:36, so Jesus now 'looks at' Peter. He looks with insight and perception.

In Matthew 16:17 Jesus calls Peter 'Simon, son of Jonah'. Here Peter is addressed as 'son of John'. Evidently there was some uncertainty about Simon's father's name. Jonah was not a very common name. If it was Simon's father's name, it might have become replaced by the more common 'John'.

Kephas is the Aramaic name which Jesus would have used, and is the equivalent of *Petros* in Greek. John is the only evangelist to use the Aramaic form, though Paul does so in 1 Corinthians and Galatians. It was not a proper name but a type of nickname, which referred to some aspect of the person. This could relate to Peter's office, or to his personality, denoting perhaps enterprise and reliability. In Matthew 16:18, where Jesus renames him, it is clearly in relation to office: 'You are Peter, and on this rock I will build my church.' In Mark 3:16 the list of the twelve that Jesus appointed simply refers to 'Simon, to whom he gave the name Peter', without any information as to when, or why, it was given. Some commentators ask whether the conferral of the new name at Jesus' first meeting with Peter is the 'reading back' of a later event.

The Call of Philip and Nathanael

v.43 The journey to Galilee may, or may not, have been in relation to the wedding to take place at 'Cana of Galilee' at John 2:1. Jesus is presumably travelling from Bethany beyond Jordan, where John was baptising (*John* 1:28).

Philip has a Gentile name (which means 'lover of horses'). He will appear at several significant points in the narrative of the Fourth Gospel. While the first two disciples had been invited with the words 'come and see' (1:39), Philip is commanded by Jesus 'follow me'.

v.44 Bethsaida, on the north-east tip of the Lake of Galilee, was technically just outside of Galilee, in Gaulanitis, the tetrarchy of Philip. It is said here to be 'the city of Andrew and Peter', though according to Mark 1:21 and 1:29 Andrew and Peter resided in Capernaum. It could be that they were born in Bethsaida, but went to live in Capernaum. The Greek name Peter (Greek *Petros*) is now used instead of the Aramaic form *Kepha*.

Other appearances of Philip in the Fourth Gospel:

6:5 Jesus said to Philip, 'Where are we to buy bread for these people to eat?'

12:21 Some Greeks came to Philip, who was from Bethsaida in Galilee, and said to him, 'Sir, we wish to see Jesus.'

14:8 Philip said to Jesus, 'Lord, show us the Father, and we will be satisfied.

On the death of Herod the Great (the Herod who figures in the opening chapters of the gospels of Matthew and Luke), who died about 4 BC, his kingdom was divided among his sons. Archelaus inherited Judaea, Samaria and Idumaea as 'ethnarch' or ruler of a people. Herod Antipas became 'tetrarch' of Galilee, and Herod Philip became 'tetrarch' in the upper Jordan region. A tetrarchy is literally a quarter of a kingdom. See Matthew 2:22 and Luke 3:1.

Plain of Bethsaida

The identification of Nathanael with Bartholomew the apostle has found its way into the liturgy. The call of Nathanael in John 1 is read on the feast of St Bartholomew on August 24th.

In Jewish tradition the Hebrew Bible comprises the Torah, the Prophets and the Writings. Torah is often translated as 'the Law' but better rendered 'teaching'. This corresponds to the books of the Pentateuch. The Prophets include books known to Christians as 'historical'. 'Writings' was a catch-all term for the remaining books of the Hebrew Bible.

St John Chrysostom writes:

Andrew was persuaded when he heard from John, and Peter was persuaded when he heard from Andrew. But Philip, not having learned anything from anyone but Christ, who said to him only this, 'Follow me,' immediately obeyed and did not go back. In fact, he even became a preacher to others.

(Homilies on the Gospel of John 20.1)

v.45 Philip is immediately acting as an apostle in finding another person to bring to Jesus. Nathanael is not mentioned in the synoptic gospels. In the Fourth Gospel, he appears only here, and at 21:2, where he is said to be 'from Cana in Galilee'. That is very interesting in view of the next narrative in the gospel taking place at Cana. Nathanael was not one of the twelve apostles, though some traditions attempted, on rather slender grounds, to identify him with Bartholomew, who is found in the lists of the twelve given in the synoptic gospels. (See *Mark 3:18*)

'Jesus son of Joseph'. The evangelist writes with irony. Jesus was not the 'son of Joseph', and the evangelist knows that the reader well knows it. This may have been how Jesus was popularly known by those who had not come to, or not yet come to, faith. As elsewhere, the evangelist does not say, and does not need to say, all that he and his readers know. At 6:42 the people ask: 'Is not this Jesus, the son of Joseph, whose father and mother we know? How can he now say: I have come down from heaven?'

Jesus is the one 'about whom Moses in the law and also the prophets wrote'. As in other instances in the New Testament, the law and the prophets are taken as representing the whole of Scripture. The third division of the Hebrew Bible, 'the writings', is not mentioned.

v.46 Nathanael was from Cana, as we learn at 21:2. His statement therefore reflects a rivalry between the two towns, Nazareth being about 15 kilometres from Cana. Nazareth is nowhere mentioned in the Old Testament, or in the early rabbinical writings, so we can talk of the 'scandal' of the Messiah coming from this obscure place. But the 'scandal' passes once the Messiah is met with faith.

Philip makes no effort to remove Nathanael's misgivings, but invites him at once to Jesus with his 'come and see', convinced that Jesus will win him over too. The 'come and see' speaks of the journey of faith. Jesus has used the same words in verse 39, to the first two disciples.

v.47 'In whom there is no deceit' may reflect the reference in Psalm 32:2 to the virtuous people 'in whose spirit is no deceit' or 'guile'.

But Jesus says that Nathanael is 'truly an Israelite in whom there is no deceit'. In the Book of Genesis, the one originally called 'Israel' was Jacob, and his deceit or cunning or guile against his brother, Esau, is narrated in Genesis chapter 27. Jesus may mean that Nathanael does not have that guile of Jacob, and is therefore more worthy of the name 'Israelite' than was Jacob.

Fig trees

v.48 The fig tree may be a symbol of the Torah. We know that it was used to symbolise the Torah in Judaism. For that reason, some add the further speculation that Nathanael may have been a scribe. Alternatively, his being under the fig tree might indicate that he was studying the Scriptures, especially the messianic prophecies, in which case, his acknowledgement of Jesus as the Messiah in verse 49 is the more understandable. Evidently the fig tree corresponds to something in Nathanael's situation, but the reference is too brief to be certain what it refers to.

With his special knowledge and sight, Jesus sees Nathanael before Philip calls him. He is said, in this gospel, to know all about people. John 2:24-25 reads: 'He knew all people, and needed no one to testify about anyone; for he himself knew what was in everyone.'

2 Samuel 7:14 I will be a father to him, and he shall be a son to me.

Psalm 2:7 You are my son; today I have begotten you.

v.49 It might seem strange to have the 'heavenly' title, 'Son of God', followed by the 'earthly' title, 'King of Israel'. The explanation might be that the 'Son of God' referred to the Davidic king (as in 2 *Samuel* 7:14 and *Psalm* 2:7) and 'King of Israel' summed up popular ideas of the messianic liberator, who would restore true kingship in Israel. The two titles would have been equivalents originally, referring to the Messiah, and confirming Philip's announcement in verse 45 that Jesus is the Messiah, 'the one about whom Moses in the law and also the prophets wrote'.

By these two titles, Nathanael recognises Jesus as the Messiah. But for the evangelist and his readers the titles have a deeper and fuller meaning of divine sonship and kingship. Thus the evangelist places

v.36	*the Lamb of God*
v.38	*Rabbi..... .which means Teacher*
v.41	*Messiah.. .which is translated Christ / Anointed*
v.45	*the one about whom Moses in the law and also the prophets wrote*
v.49	*Son of God ... King of Israel*
v.51	*the Son of Man upon whom the angels of God ascend and descend*

'Son of God' first, to express the predominantly religious meaning of messiahship.

v.50 Nathaniel will see 'greater things' in the signs of Jesus, from Cana onwards.

v.51 'Very truly, I tell you'. The Jerusalem Bible translates, 'I tell you most solemnly'. Literally, it is 'Amen, Amen. I say to you.' The use of this phrase as the preface to a statement is unknown in Jewish writings, and is possibly unique to Jesus. The double 'Amen' form occurs only in John's gospel, where it is used twenty-five times. The single form with just one 'Amen', 'truly I tell you' in the New Revised Standard Version Bible, occurs frequently in the sayings of Jesus in the synoptic gospels.

There are several indications that this verse is an independent saying of Jesus that has been placed here. There is a new introduction, 'And he said to him', and the 'you' is now plural. The saying is in effect a repetition, or variant, of the promise in verse 50 of seeing greater things. It is a unique saying in the Fourth Gospel, as there is nowhere else mention of angels as intermediaries between the Son of Man on earth and God in heaven.

The background of the saying is found in the Genesis story of Jacob's ladder. Genesis 28:12-13 reads: 'and he (Jacob) dreamed that there was a ladder set upon the earth, and the top of it reached to heaven; and behold the angels of God were ascending and descending upon it' (or 'upon him'). In Jesus' saying the angels are ascending and descending 'upon the Son of Man', rather than upon the ladder.

The meaning of the saying is that the Son of Man is now the connection between heavenly and earthly reality, replacing Bethel, where Jacob's experience happened, or Israel, as the place of God's dwelling. This is a unique statement in the Fourth Gospel, but in many ways it can be regarded as the key to all that Jesus does and is, according to this gospel. The disciples are promised in Jesus a spiritual insight comparable to Jacob's vision.

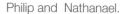
Philip and Nathanael.

The Word Lives On

In the Lectionary

The call of the first three disciples (*John* 1:35-42) is read on the 2nd Sunday in Ordinary Time in Year B. It is also read during the Christmas Season on 4th January.

The call of Philip and Nathanael (*John* 1:43-51) is read during the Christmas Season on 5th January, and the call of Nathanael (*John* 1:45-51) on the Feast of St Bartholomew (August 24th).

Live the Word of God

Listen once more to the reading.

What do you hear now?

Suggestions for reflection and prayer

What are the features of the call of Peter in the Fourth Gospel?

Reflect on the words of Bede given in the margin.

What strikes you about the call of Nathanael?

From the Venerable Bede:

From John's disciples Jesus summoned two to follow him, and one of them, Andrew, led his brother Peter to him also. According to the spiritual sense, it is clear what it means to follow the Lord. You follow the Lord if you imitate him. You follow the Lord if, insofar as human weakness allows, you do not abandon those examples of humility that, as a human being, the Son of God demonstrated. You follow the Lord if, by showing yourself to be a companion of his sufferings, you painstakingly long to attain communion in his resurrection and ascension.

(Homilies on the Gospels 1.17)

The Venerable Bede

Jesus invites the first disciples to 'come and see'.

❖ Pray for a spirit of hospitality and welcome in our Christian communities.

Andrew brings Simon to Jesus, and Philip brings Nathanael.

❖ Pray that we may lead others to Christ and his Church.

Peter is called Kephas, the rock.

❖ Pray for constancy amid the trials of being a disciple of Jesus.

Nathanael is promised the vision of 'greater things'.

❖ Pray for an openness to God's surprises.

Statue of St. Peter in Rome (Vatican).

The Wedding at Cana in Galilee

Hear the Word of God

Read John 2:1-11

[1] On the third day, there was a wedding in Cana of Galilee, and the mother of Jesus was there.

[2] Jesus and his disciples had also been invited to the wedding.

[3] When the wine gave out, the mother of Jesus said to him, 'They have no wine.'

[4] And Jesus said to her, 'Woman, what concern is that to you and to me? My hour has not yet come.' [5] His mother said to the servants, 'Do whatever he tells you.'

[6] Now standing there were six stone water-jars for the Jewish rites of purification, each holding twenty or thirty gallons. [7] Jesus said to them, 'Fill the jars with water.' And they filled them to the brim. [8] He said to them, 'Now draw some out, and take it to the chief steward.' So they took it.

[9] When the steward tasted the water that had become wine, and did not know where it came from (though the servants who had drawn the water knew), the steward called the bridegroom [10] and said to him, 'Everyone serves the good wine first, and then the inferior wine after the guests have become drunk. But you have kept the good wine until now.'

[11] Jesus did this, the first of his signs, in Cana of Galilee, and revealed his glory; and his disciples believed in him.

Opposite: Wedding at Cana by Dinah Roe Kendall.

Understand the Word of God

This session will explore:
- ❖ the meaning of the first sign of Jesus
- ❖ the role of the mother of Jesus
- ❖ the developing faith of the disciples
- ❖ the idea of the 'glory' of Jesus

Setting in the Gospel

This passage follows immediately after the previous one we looked at, and completes the counting of the days of the first week. The sequence of days began in 1:19 when John the Baptist gave his testimony about himself. On the next day in 1:29 John first pointed to Jesus as the 'Lamb of God'. On the third and fourth days, in 1:35 and 1:43, Jesus encountered his first disciples. Our passage now completes the sequence of days with the phrase 'on the third day' in 2:1, which introduces the story of the first sign.

Cretan water jars.

What Kind of Text?

This narrative is found only in the Fourth Gospel. It is a miracle narrative, except that John never employs the synoptic term 'miracle', or 'mighty act', but rather the designation 'sign' (Greek *semeion*). While the evangelist does not define for us what he means by a 'sign', the term evidently refers to the power of God working in Jesus.

This event at Cana is said by the evangelist to be 'the first' or 'the beginning' of the signs of Jesus (1:11), and he tells us quite clearly at the end of his writing, in 20:30-31, that he gives us in his gospel only a selection of the signs Jesus did, and that faith and life are the purpose in recounting them.

All of the signs are extraordinary. In fact, they seem to go from the extraordinary to the more extraordinary, in an increasing crescendo. At Cana, a colossal amount of wine, one hundred and twenty to one hundred and eighty gallons, is produced by the mere word of Jesus. Similarly with the second Cana sign, where Jesus remains at Cana, the sick boy who is restored is eight miles away at Capernaum.

In the third sign, the crippled man has presumably been lying unhelped at the Pool of Bethzatha for a very long time, for the evangelist tells us that he has been ill for 38 years (5:5). The crowd of five thousand in Galilee are fed with just five barley loaves and two fishes. That evening Jesus walks on the waters towards his disciples in the boat. No wonder they are terrified (6:19).

The man who is given sight was not just blind for a time, but born blind. Lazarus is not just dead, but well and truly dead and buried: 'already in the tomb for four days' (11:17) such that, as the old translations put it, 'he stinketh' (11:39). It is of course this last sign of his ministry that most closely points to the greatest sign that Jesus would give, his resurrection from the dead.

John 20:30-31 reads:

Now Jesus did many other signs in the presence of his disciples, which are not written in this book. But these are written so that you may believe that Jesus is the Messiah, the Son of God, and that through believing you may have life in his name.

The Seven Signs in the ministry of Jesus

2:1-11 the marriage at Cana in Galilee

4:46-54 the second Cana sign: the healing of the official's son

5:1-18 the healing of the crippled man

6:1-14 the feeding of five thousand

6:16-21 the walking on the waters

9:1-41 the giving of sight to the man born blind

11:1-53 the raising of Lazarus.

Commentary: verse by verse reading

The Setting of the Scene

v.1 'On the third day' marks the end of Jesus' 'inaugural' week of ministry, in which he gathered his disciples, and the start of the second week of ministry in earnest. An allusion to his resurrection from the dead is unlikely, in that John, unlike Acts and St Paul, does not use the expression 'on the third day' in reference to the resurrection of Jesus.

The Fourth Gospel is the only New Testament writing to mention Cana, which we hear about again at 4:46, at the healing of the official's son. It is again mentioned at 21:2, where we are told that Nathanael came from there. The Jewish historian Josephus mentions Cana several times in connection with the Jewish Revolt against Roman rule in 66-67AD. Ancient Cana is probably Khirbet Qana, some 10 miles north of Nazareth, and not Kefr Kenna, to which pilgrims are usually taken.

'The mother of Jesus' is never given the name 'Mary' in the Fourth Gospel. It is probably deliberate, significant and symbolic that both here, and in the other passage where she occurs, 19:25-27, she is referred to as 'the mother of Jesus' rather than 'Mary', and addressed by Jesus as 'Woman'.

vv.2-3 It seems that Jesus and the disciples arrived later at the wedding, though it is not explicitly indicated. 'They have no wine' is merely a statement by the mother of Jesus. It is not an explicit request, even if it is implicitly one. The explanation that they ran out of wine because Jesus' rowdy disciples arrived and drank the lot has some humour about it, but is not warranted by anything the evangelist has written.

vv.4-5 'What concern is that to you and to me?' is literally in the Greek of the gospel 'What to me and to you?' This form of speaking could be a hostile rebuke, as, for example, when in Mark's story of the healing of the possessed man in the synagogue at Capernaum the demons say to Jesus 'What have you to do with us, Jesus of Nazareth?' (*Mark* 1:24). In the Cana story it is more likely to express disinterest, or disengagement, as in the expression 'What has it got to do with us?'

The 'hour' of Jesus is his glorification, seen by the evangelist in his passion, death and resurrection. Since Jesus will go on to perform further signs after this one, and in advance of his hour, this explanation does not make great sense of his apparent unwillingness to intervene.

'Woman' is a most unusual address of a Jewish son for his mother, even if it was a respectful address for a woman one did not know, as we see in the words of Jesus to the Samaritan woman at 4:21. Jesus hardly addresses his mother in this way in coldness towards her, or for that matter in deference to her. As with the use of this address by Jesus from the cross at 19:26, 'woman' probably evokes the 'woman' of salvation history. Is the evangelist suggesting that the role of this woman, Mary, is comparable to that of the first woman, Eve? Later commentators certainly thought so.

Eve was 'the mother of all who live' (*Genesis* 3:20). Mary is the mother of the Messiah and called 'mother of Jesus' by the evangelist. From the cross, when his 'hour' comes, he will make her the mother of his disciple(s). Evidently Jesus' addressing his mother as 'woman' was important for its theological symbolism to the evangelist and his community.

'What to me and to you?' is in fact an expression found in the Hebrew of the Old Testament. When the prophet Elijah meets the widow of Zarephath, whose son is gravely ill, she cries out to Elijah with the words 'What to me and to you, man of God?' The sense here is something like 'What have you against me, man of God?'
The story, in 1 Kings 17:17-24, ends with the boy's healing.

Some more texts about the 'hour':
8:20 He spoke these words while he was teaching in the treasury of the temple, but no one arrested him, because his hour had not yet come.
12:23 Jesus answered them, 'The hour has come for the Son of Man to be glorified.'
13:1 Now before the festival of the Passover, Jesus knew that his hour had come to depart from this world and go to the Father.

In the Book of Revelation chapter 12 the dragon makes war on 'the woman' who gives birth to a male son. In this case 'the woman' is primarily not the mother of Jesus, but Israel as mother of the Messiah. The reading is used on the feast of the Assumption of Mary, which celebrates her being taken body and soul into the life of the resurrection. The woman is presented in glory in the opening verses of the chapter.

The Working of the Sign

v.6 One hundred and twenty or one hundred and eighty gallons, or six to seven hundred litres, are involved. A huge amount of wine is going to be provided. It suggests the abundance of wine at the Messiah's coming and the messianic banquet. There are not many Old Testament texts that are explicit on this specific theme, though Joel 3:18 and Amos 9:13 can be invoked.

Since the stone water-jars are 'for the Jewish rites of purification', does this signify that the 'good' and plentiful wine brought by the Messiah, and 'kept until now' (verse 10), replaces the water of Judaism? Since replacement, or fulfilment, by Jesus of the institutions of Judaism is a prominent theme of this gospel, it is not impossible that this is intended.

Alternatively, is 'for the Jewish rites of purification' a purely incidental, insignificant narrative detail? This is unlikely in the Fourth Gospel. A further suggestion of some of the Fathers, that the number 'six' indicates imperfection, because it is one less than seven, the perfect number, is less certain. Unlike in the Apocalypse, series of numbers are not prominent in the Fourth Gospel. In addition, is there a deeper meaning in 'they have no wine' in verse 3? Is it a statement about the barrenness of Jewish ceremonial before the coming of the Messiah?

vv.7-10 The evangelist explains to the reader that even the steward of the feast did not realise what had been done: only the servants and, by implication, the mother of Jesus and his disciples, knew what really happened. The miraculous is narrated in a discreet, 'quiet' way, in 'behind the scenes' action. On this basis, we can say that the focus here is not so much on the miraculous as on its significance, on its value as a 'sign'.

As a narrative, the account is incomplete in many ways. For example, we are never told who the bride and the groom were, what their reaction to what took place was, or why Jesus and his mother and his disciples were there at the wedding celebration. As elsewhere with the Fourth Gospel, such points are not important for the evangelist's purposes.

Amos 9:13 The mountains shall drip sweet wine, and all the hills shall flow with it.

Joel 3:18 In that day the mountains shall drip sweet wine, the hills shall flow with milk, and all the streambeds of Judah shall flow with water.

In his encyclical letter on Mary, published in 1987 and entitled 'The Mother of the Redeemer' (Redemptoris Mater), Pope John Paul II wrote:

At Cana, thanks to the intercession of Mary and the obedience of the servants, Jesus begins 'his hour'.

At Cana Mary appears as believing in Jesus. Her faith evokes his first 'sign' and helps to kindle the faith of the disciples. (21)

v.11 'The first of his signs' is literally 'the beginning of the signs' (Greek *he arche ton semeion*). Only the first two signs, both at Cana, are counted off, in 2:11 and 4:54.

Jesus 'revealed' or 'manifested his glory'. This 'glory' is his as the only Son of the Father. So we are told in John 1:14. What later theology would call the 'divinity' of Jesus is expressed in the Fourth Gospel as his 'glory'. John 12:23 states that it is in the 'hour' of Jesus that his glory is revealed. Remember how Jesus said to his mother at 2:4, 'My hour has not yet come'. We are probably therefore to think of the glory of Jesus revealed at Cana as a partial manifestation, or a foretaste, of his glory, awaiting the fulness of its revealing upon the cross. The cross is the true event of glory in the Fourth Gospel.

The Marriage at Cana, (1723) by Bartolomeo Litterini, (1669-1745)

'His disciples believed in him.' The tense of the verb is the Greek aorist, which indicates that it means 'they came to believe in him'. This is their first act of faith in him. In their first week with Jesus, their 'formation' as disciples has been completed, even though they have much to learn and to understand. They have been called by Jesus, responded to him by coming to and staying with him, and have now come to faith in him.

The sign given at Cana was a unique miracle. It was not to relieve pain or illness, or to give life to the dead. It does not neatly compare to the feeding of the five thousand, where the motive was the alleviation of hunger. The provision of wine, although saving the day for the wedding guests, and saving the embarrassment of the couple, has more to do with celebration and enjoyment.

The Second Vatican Council, in its Dogmatic Constitution on the Church, entitled Lumen Gentium, has this to say about Mary and the wedding at Cana:

In the public life of Jesus, Mary makes significant appearances. This is so even at the very beginning, when at the marriage feast of Cana, moved with pity, she brought about by her intercession the beginning of miracles of Jesus the Messiah. (58)

The Marriage at Cana, Bohemian School (17th century)

The Word Lives On

In the Liturgy and the Lectionary

This account of the wedding at Cana has long been associated with the Christmas season. Although Jesus is obviously an adult and has already gathered his disciples, the text is linked with the story of the Epiphany as a 'manifestation' of the glory of Jesus. Together with the story of the Baptism of the Lord these three traditions became associated with each other as 'revelations' or 'manifestations' of the true identity of Jesus.

The antiphon sung before and after the *Magnificat* at Second Vespers for the feast of the Epiphany reads as follows: 'Three wonders mark this day we celebrate: today the star led the Magi to the manger; today water was changed into wine at the marriage feast; today Christ desired to be baptised by John in the river Jordan to bring us salvation. Alleluia.'

This extraordinary gathering of the mysteries of Christ is echoed in the mysteries of the rosary. While there is no explicit reference to the magi, it can be included in the third Joyful Mystery of the Birth of Our Lord. The Baptism of Jesus and the first Cana miracle are included in the Luminous Mysteries promulgated by Pope John Paul II.

Unfortunately, in the three-year cycle of readings the narrative of the Wedding at Cana is only read on the Second Sunday in Ordinary Time in Year C. Interestingly, the first reading chosen to accompany the gospel on this Sunday speaks of the wedding of God to Israel (*Isaiah* 62:1-5). The Wedding at Cana is also a popular reading for marriage services.

Other Interpretations

Those who have commented on the story of the wedding at Cana throughout the Christian centuries have realised that the significance of the narrative is unquestionably Christological. It is about the uniqueness of Jesus, about the manifestation of his 'glory', which is seen only by those with the eyes to see, and about the faith of his disciples.

The story of the first Cana sign was not written to teach about the power of the prayerful intercession of the mother of Jesus on our behalf. Despite its usage for this purpose by some preachers, it is hard to imagine such a theology being the evangelist's purpose.

Some interpreters have asked whether there is a sacramental symbolism in this narrative. It is indeed the moment of the disciples' coming to faith, but it is not easy to see a reference to Baptism, when the water at Cana is made into wine. Neither is it easy to see a reference to the Eucharist, when there is no mention of bread. Despite the popularity of this passage as the gospel reading at wedding liturgies, being the only gospel account of the presence of Jesus at a wedding celebration, it is not easy to see an intended reference to the sacrament of marriage. The narrative makes no mention of the couple or of their wedding ceremony.

St John Chrysostom explains why Jesus attended the wedding:

Since our Lord was known in Galilee, they invite him to the marriage. And he comes because he cares more about our good than his own dignity. The one who did not despise taking on himself the form of a servant would much less despise being present at the marriage of servants.

(Homilies on the Gospel of John 21.1)

Modern day Cana, southern end.

Live the Word of God

Listen once more to the reading.

What do you hear now?
Suggestions for reflection and prayer

Why does this evangelist refer to the miracles of Jesus as signs?

Reflect on the text from Maximus of Turin given on the next page.

How does John's presentation of the mother of Jesus in this account strike you?

The disciples gradually become more aware of the 'glory' of Jesus, which is fully revealed when the 'hour' of his passion, death and resurrection arrives.

❖ Pray for the patience to know Jesus gradually through prayer and Christian life.

The mother of Jesus is supportive of Jesus and his disciples.

❖ Pray for all parents that they may foster the maturity of their children.

Jesus' coming brings to fulfilment the teachings and prophecies of the Jewish Scriptures.

❖ Pray for insight to appreciate how God's revelation unfolds in the Scriptures of Old and New Testament.

St Maximus, who was born about 380, was the first bishop of Turin. He comments:

The Son of God went to a wedding so that marriage, which had been instituted by his own authority, might be sanctified by his blessed presence. He went to a wedding of the old order when he was about to take a new bride for himself through the conversion of the Gentiles, a bride who would forever remain a virgin. He went to a wedding even though he himself was not born of human wedlock. He went to a wedding not to enjoy a banquet but rather to make himself known by miracles. He went to a wedding not to drink wine but to give it, for when there was none left for the wedding guests, the most blessed Mary said to him: They have no wine.

(Sermon 23)

The Wedding at Cana by JesusMafa.

Jesus and Nicodemus

Hear the Word of God

Read John 3:1-15

[1] Now there was a Pharisee named Nicodemus, a leader of the Jews. [2] He came to Jesus by night and said to him, 'Rabbi, we know that you are a teacher who has come from God; for no one can do these signs that you do apart from the presence of God.' [3] Jesus answered him, 'Very truly, I tell you, no one can see the kingdom of God without being born from above.' [4] Nicodemus said to him, 'How can anyone be born after having grown old? Can one enter a second time into the mother's womb and be born?' [5] Jesus answered, 'Very truly, I tell you, no one can enter the kingdom of God without being born of water and Spirit. [6] What is born of the flesh is flesh, and what is born of the Spirit is spirit. [7] Do not be astonished that I said to you, 'You must be born from above.' [8] The wind blows where it chooses, and you hear the sound of it, but you do not know where it comes from, or where it goes. So it is with everyone who is born of the Spirit.' [9] Nicodemus said to him, 'How can these things be?' [10] Jesus answered him, 'Are you a teacher of Israel, and yet you do not understand these things?

[11] 'Very truly, I tell you, we speak of what we know, and testify to what we have seen; yet you do not receive our testimony. [12] If I have told you about earthly things and you do not believe, how can you believe if I tell you about heavenly things? [13] No one has ascended into heaven except the one who descended from heaven, the Son of Man. [14] And just as Moses lifted up the serpent in the wilderness, so must the Son of Man be lifted up, [15] that whoever believes in him may have eternal life.'

Opposite: Christ Talks with Nicodemus, illustration for 'The Life of Christ', c.1886-94. By James Tissot (1836-1902).

Understand the Word of God

This session will explore:

❖ the role of Nicodemus

❖ what it means to be 'born from above'

❖ the idea of 'wind' and 'spirit'

Setting in the Gospel

Following the sign at Cana in Galilee, and a stay of a few days in Capernaum (2:12), Jesus goes to Jerusalem where he 'cleanses' the temple (2:13-22). Though we are told nothing explicitly, the conversation with Nicodemus apparently also takes place in Jerusalem.

Nicodemus by Jesus Mafa.

What Kind of Text?

This passage has sometimes been referred to as a 'dialogue' with Nicodemus, but this does not seem to be an accurate description. Nicodemus makes only a few interventions by way of questions that show his incomprehension but allow Jesus to continue teaching and explaining. A better description of our text might be 'Discourse of Jesus, with some questions from Nicodemus'.

A rough division of the whole passage, of which we are considering the first fifteen verses, could be: vv. 3-8 on the Spirit; vv. 11-15 on the Son of Man and vv. 16-21 on God's sending of his Son. At some point, Nicodemus drops out of the narrative, possibly after verse 12.

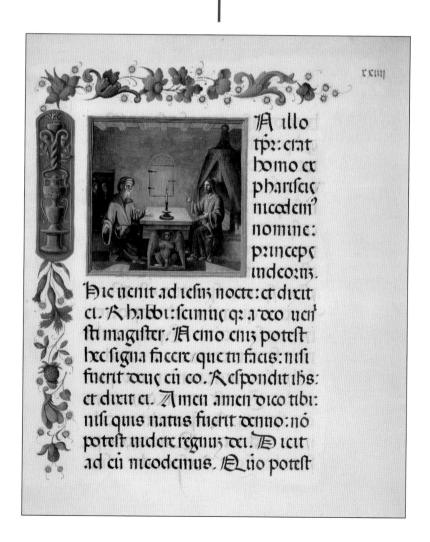

Christ and Nicodemus from the Evangelarium of Santa Giustina written by Laurentius Gazius Cremonensis, 1523-25.

Commentary: verse by verse reading

Born of the Spirit

v.1 There are three descriptions of Nicodemus in this passage. He is referred to first of all as a Pharisee. Then he is called a leader, literally 'ruler', of the Jews, which could imply that he was a member of the Sanhedrin, the governing council of the Jewish leaders. In verse 10 Nicodemus is called a 'teacher in Israel'.

He will have two other appearances in this gospel. At 7:50-52 he will take the side of Jesus, insisting that the Jewish law 'does not judge people, without first giving them a hearing, to find out what they are doing'. At 19:39 Nicodemus will bring one hundred pounds of myrrh and aloes for the burial of Jesus.

He clearly represents official Judaism, the 'Pharisaism' of the evangelist's day. Some have asked whether Nicodemus is purely an imaginary, representative character, serving as a foil against whom Jesus presents his teaching, and therefore not to be regarded as a historical person. But this does not exclude the possibility of his being historical.

v.2 His coming to Jesus by night was presumably to avoid being seen and attracting notice. At 13:30, when Judas departs from the supper table, the evangelist states tersely 'and it was night'. The symbolism there, of the reign of darkness, does not apply here. Probably the meaning here concerns Nicodemus coming out of the darkness to the Light, who is Jesus.

In Jewish tradition, night time was recommended for the study of the Torah, and the rabbis often prolonged their teaching and discussion well into the night. Nicodemus refers to Jesus as 'Rabbi', just as the disciples had done in 1:38.

'We know that you are a teacher who has come from God'. There may be some polite exaggeration here. Do the other Jewish teachers also share this opinion? Evidently Nicodemus represents a Judaism that is receptive to Jesus. He gives a positive appraisal of Jesus: that he is a

---

A traditional rabbinic saying reads:

Whoever learns Torah at night is granted grace during the day and whoever neglects it will be fed burning coals in the world to come.
(Avodah Zarah 3b)

Maimonides, one of the greatest sages of Jewish history, wrote:

Although it is a religious duty to study day and night, most of a person's knowledge is gained only during night-time. Whoever studies Torah at night, a touch of grace lights his face at daytime.

(Tikkun Leil Shavuot)

teacher come from God, and that the signs he gives indicate God's presence with him.

The evangelist emphasises Jesus' teaching about what is necessary for salvation. The Judaism of the day was seriously concerned with this question, as we see from questions asked of Jesus in the synoptic tradition. The rich young man asks, 'What must I do to attain eternal life?' (*Mark* 10:17) The lawyer enquires, 'What is the most important commandment?' (*Mark* 12:28). Since Jesus' answer in verse 3 speaks of 'the kingdom', Nicodemus may well have had in mind a similar question, which has not been preserved in the gospel tradition, about inheriting salvation and the kingdom of God.

v.3 The unusual expression 'to see the kingdom of God' has the same meaning as the more usual 'to enter the kingdom'

Visit of Nicodemus to Christ, 1880 by John La Farge, (1835-1910)'

that occurs in sayings of Jesus in the synoptic gospels. 'To see the kingdom' can be understood as to experience it. The expression 'kingdom of God' is rare in the Fourth Gospel. It occurs only here, in verse 3 and 5. At 18:36 Jesus says to Pilate: 'my kingship (kingdom) is not of this world.'

What does the phrase 'without being born from above' mean? The Greek original can be translated both 'born' and 'begotten'. (The male 'begets', while the female 'bears'.)

The Greek word *anothen* used here can mean both 'from above' and 'again'. It is a deliberate word-play, which causes Nicodemus' apparently silly confusion in verse 4. The fact that it is a Greek word-play, which is not possible in Aramaic or Hebrew, the languages Jesus would have spoken, raises the question whether it is creative writing by the evangelist rather than historical words of Jesus.

Other uses of the word in the gospel indicate that 'from above' (rather than 'again') is the intended meaning. The same thought of birth or begetting from God 'from above' has already been expressed in the Prologue at 1:13, concerning those 'who were born not of blood, or of the will of the flesh or of the will of man, but of God'.

Early Christian theology provided two different explanations for the divine sonship that God bestows on humans. In some New Testament writings, it is explained as begetting or procreation, while St Paul explains it as adoption.

v.4 Misunderstanding is frequently used in the Gospel of John, usually prompting further explanation or teaching from Jesus. Nicodemus' question 'How can anyone be born after having grown old?' comes across as a crass misunderstanding. It has been caused by the double meanings of the two expressions Jesus has used. Nicodemus seems to think that to be born again has to be understood in a physical way.

Nicodemus' only contributions to the exchange are his positive statement about Jesus in verse 2, his questions in verse 4, and his further question in verse 9, 'how can these things be?'

v.5 In this verse we have 'enter the kingdom of God', while in verse 3 we had 'see the kingdom of God'. There seems to be little difference. We can also ask whether 'begotten' or 'born of water and the spirit' refers to baptism. Christian baptism was not instituted by Jesus during his ministry, but we find it commanded by Jesus after his resurrection in Matthew 28:19.

Despite the reference to water here, the evangelist is focusing on the new creation by God's spirit, rather than on the sacrament of baptism.

v.6 'Flesh', as used in St Paul, denotes inherent human sinfulness, but this is not the meaning in John, where it denotes human weakness and mortality. In John it is not therefore an unmistakably 'bad' word as it is in St Paul.

For John, there is an essential difference between the two realms of being, 'flesh' and 'spirit'. It is impossible for the human to attain the kingdom by his or her own powers. Because of earthly birth, the human belongs to the realm of the 'flesh'. The divine and heavenly world of 'spirit' is beyond his reach by his own powers.

vv.7-8 These verses contain something like a short parable, as is evident from the 'so it is' towards the end. The Spirit is compared to the wind. Once again we have words with more than one meaning. The word translated 'sound' (Greek *phone*) can also mean 'voice'. The word translated 'wind' (Greek *pneuma*) can also mean 'spirit'. The 'sound of the wind' can therefore also mean the 'voice of the spirit'.

'So it is with everyone who is born of the Spirit'. All those begotten, or born, of the Spirit hear or experience it, but are unable to explain its workings. The supernatural process is mysterious and impenetrable of its very nature, invisible to the human. The implication is that Nicodemus should abandon his questioning and believe.

v.9 This is Nicodemus' third intervention, and as in verse 4 it expresses lack of understanding and incredulity. It may also represent the incredulity of the Jews of the evangelist's day (late first century) towards the Christian proclamation.

v.10 A teacher like Nicodemus should have grasped what Jesus meant by birth from the Spirit. There were, after all, various Scripture texts that spoke of the action of the Spirit in the last days. The words may sound like sarcasm on Jesus' part, but perhaps they represent the frustration of the Church in trying to address the Jews, and not being heard.

The Catechism of the Catholic Church says this about being born of the Spirit:

To become a child in relation to God is the condition of entering the kingdom. For this, we must humble ourselves and become little. Even more: to become 'children of God' we must be 'born from above' or 'born of God'. Only when Christ is formed in us will the mystery of Christmas be fulfilled in us. Christmas is the mystery of this 'marvellous exchange'.

(526)

Joel 2:28-29 (3:1-2) reads:

Then afterward I will pout out my spirit on all flesh; your sons and your daughters shall prophesy, your old men shall dream dreams, and your young men shall see visions. Even on the male and female slaves, in those days, I will pour out my spirit.

The Son of Man

v.11 The plural 'we' sounds like the proclamation of the apostolic preaching in the early Church, and the word 'testimony' would support this. Jesus is portrayed as associating himself with his later disciples who will preach the Christian gospel. The 'you' in verses 11-12 is in the plural, and sounds like the Church addressing the Jews, but to no avail.

v.12 The distinction between 'earthly things' and 'heavenly things' may perhaps mean that Jesus has so far talked about 'earthly' things such as birth, sound, and wind.

Paul in 1 Corinthians 3:1-2 makes a similar distinction, when he writes about the 'milk' he gives to those he calls 'people of the flesh', and the 'solid food' he would give to 'spiritual people'. In this passage we have no idea what the 'heavenly things' Jesus speaks of are. Jesus understandably does not go on to explain them to the uncomprehending Nicodemus, who has failed to understand even the basic fundamentals, the 'earthly things'.

v.13 The implication in Jesus' words that the Son of Man has already ascended into heaven gave difficulty to some of the early scribes who copied this gospel by hand. They added the words 'who is in heaven' to the end of the verse (producing 'the Son of Man who is in heaven') in an unsuccessful attempt to clarify the meaning. These scribes probably had in mind a bodily ascension of Jesus, as depicted in Luke 24:51 and Acts 1:6-11.

However, 'descending' and 'ascending' are words used by this evangelist for the Redeemer's coming to earth and returning to his Father. They have their own meaning here, which has nothing to do with Luke's picture of a physical assumption or ascension. For John, the ascent of the Son of Man will be accomplished in his future glorification, the 'hour' of his death and resurrection.

Some suggest that the 'no one has ascended into heaven' statement is directed against apocalyptic visionaries, Gnostics or others, who claimed to have gone up to heaven, and there received heavenly revelations. The meaning is clear that no one other than the Son of Man has been in heaven and therefore no one but he is able to bring down to earth knowledge of heavenly things.

v.14 There are three statements in this gospel about the 'lifting up' of the Son of Man. In addition to our present passage, in John 8:28 Jesus says: 'When you have lifted up the Son of Man, then you will know that I am he.' These words are understood to allude to the divine name 'I am' in Exodus 3:14. In 12:32 he says, 'and I, when I am lifted up from the earth, will draw all people to myself.' In the following verse the evangelist explains that Jesus 'said this to indicate the kind of death he was to die'.

The Volto Santo, Italian School, (12th century)

By coincidence the synoptic gospels have three predictions by Jesus of his passion and death, but they are phrased quite differently. John's statements about being 'lifted up' imply the crucifixion, and the question is asked whether Jesus foretold his death in this vivid way, or whether the statements were phrased in this way after his death and resurrection.

It needs to be said that the 'lifting up' of the Son of Man is more than just his crucifixion. It is also his glorification, since crucifixion alone did not draw all people to him (12:32), or bring them to realise that 'I am he' (8:28). The Fourth Evangelist does not speak of a passion and death which are a humiliation, as they are in the synoptic gospels. For John, the 'scandal of the cross', to use St Paul's term (*Galatians* 5:11), is not overcome just by the subsequent resurrection, but redeemed by the majesty and saving power of the cross itself. It is quite true to say that the crucifixion is so rich in John's thought as to immediately imply glory and glorification.

When Jesus says 'just as Moses lifted up the serpent in the wilderness' there are two points of comparison with the bronze serpent fashioned by Moses in the Book of Numbers to heal the people from poisonous serpents. These points of comparison are the lifting up, and life as the consequence. Numbers 21:9 reads: 'So Moses made a serpent of bronze, and put it upon a pole; and whenever a serpent bit someone, that person would look at the serpent of bronze and live'.

v.15 Rather than 'that whoever believes in him may have eternal life' we should probably better translate 'that whoever believes may have eternal life in him.' This is because 'believing in him' is usually expressed in Greek by 'into him' (*eis auton*) rather than 'in him' (*en auto*), which is the reading of this verse in the best manuscript tradition. A similar idea is found in John 20:31, where we read: 'These are written so that you may come to believe that Jesus is the Messiah, the Son of God, and that through believing you may have life in his name.'

St Bede comments:

Just as those who looked at the bronze serpent that had been lifted up as a sign were cured at that time from temporal death and the wounds that the serpents' bites had caused, so too those who look at the mystery of the Lord's passion by believing, confessing and sincerely imitating it are saved for ever from every death they have incurred by sinning in mind and body.

(Homilies on the Gospels 2.18)

The Word Lives On

In the Lectionary

John 3 speaks of new life through being born from above in the Spirit. It is therefore no surprise that we read from this chapter at the beginning of the Easter season, when we celebrate the new life given through the resurrection of Christ. Our passage, John 3:1-15, is read at Mass on the Monday and Tuesday of the second week of Easter.

The reference to the 'Son of Man being lifted up' in verse 14 suggests that our text might also be relevant to the season of Lent. On the Fourth Sunday of Lent in Year B the gospel reading is John 3:14-21.

Nicodemus Visits Christ by the Italian School, (15th century).

Live the Word of God

Good Friday intercession for the Jewish people:

Let us pray for the Jewish people, the first to hear the word of God, that they may continue to grow in the love of his name and in faithfulness to his covenant.

Listen once more to the reading.

What do you hear now?
Suggestions for reflection and prayer

How much progress does Nicodemus make on the journey of faith?

Reflect on the Good Friday intercession for the Jewish People, given in the margin.

How can a Christian make the progression from 'earthly things' to 'heavenly things'?

Baptismal font.

Nicodemus makes slow progress towards faith in Jesus.

❖ Pray for openness to heavenly realities and the things of the Spirit.

Christians are born again in baptism by water and the Spirit.

❖ Pray for those preparing to be baptised and for those who support them.

In being 'lifted up' Jesus draws all people to himself.

❖ Pray for the willingness to be drawn by Jesus into newness of life.

Nicodemus represents Judaism and its difficulties with Christian beliefs.

❖ Pray for the Jewish people, the first to be called the 'people of God'.

People praying at the Western Wall, Jerusalem, Israel.

Jesus and the Samaritan Woman

Hear the Word of God

Read John 4:5-26

5 Jesus came to a Samaritan town called Sychar, near the plot of ground that Jacob had given his son Joseph. 6 Jacob's well was there, and Jesus, tired out by his journey, was sitting by the well. It was about noon.

7 A Samaritan woman came to draw water, and Jesus said to her, 'Give me a drink.' 8 (His disciples had gone to the city to buy food.) 9 The Samaritan woman said to him, 'How is it that you, a Jew, ask a drink of me, a woman of Samaria?' (Jews do not share things in common with Samaritans.)

10 Jesus answered her, 'If you knew the gift of God, and who it is that is saying to you, 'Give me a drink', you would have asked him, and he would have given you living water.' 11 The woman said to him, 'Sir, you have no bucket, and the well is deep. Where do you get that living water? 12 Are you greater than our ancestor Jacob, who gave us this well, and with his sons and his flocks drank from it?' 13 Jesus said to her, 'Everyone who drinks of this water will be thirsty again, 14 but those who drink of the water that I will give them will never be thirsty. The water that I will give will become in them a spring of water gushing up to eternal life.' 15 The woman said to him, 'Sir, give me this water, so that I may never be thirsty or have to keep coming here to draw water.'

16 Jesus said to her, 'Go, call your husband, and come back.' 17 The woman answered him, 'I have no husband.' Jesus said to her, 'You are right in saying, 'I have no husband'; 18 for you have had five husbands, and the one you have now is not your husband. What you have said is true!'

19 The woman said to him, 'Sir, I see that you are a prophet. 20 Our ancestors worshipped on this mountain, but you say that the place where people must worship is in Jerusalem.' 21 Jesus said to her, 'Woman, believe me, the hour is coming when you will worship the Father neither on this mountain nor in Jerusalem. 22 You worship what you do not know; we worship what we know, for salvation is from the Jews. 23 But the hour is coming, and is now here, when the true worshippers will worship the Father in spirit and truth, for the Father seeks such as these to worship him. 24 God is spirit, and those who worship him must worship in spirit and truth.' 25 The woman said to him, 'I know that Messiah is coming' (who is called Christ). 'When he comes, he will proclaim all things to us.' 26 Jesus said to her, 'I am he, the one who is speaking to you.'

Opposite: Christ and the Woman of Samaria by Juan de Flandres, (c.1465-1519)

Understand the Word of God

This session will explore:

- ❖ Jesus' treatment of the Samaritan woman
- ❖ her reaction to Jesus
- ❖ the idea of worship 'in spirit and in truth'

Setting in the Gospel

The conversation with Nicodemus, which we left at 3:15, is presumed to have taken place in Jerusalem. Further discourse of Jesus followed, with a discussion between John the Baptist and his disciples in 3:25-30, containing the Baptist's last words of testimony to the Messiah, 'He must increase, but I must decrease.' (3:30)

Jesus at Jacob's Well by John Millar Watt.

The opening verses of chapter 4 speak of Jesus returning from Judaea to Galilee and passing through Samaria. We take up the story with the arrival of Jesus in Sychar. After our passage, the story will continue with the return of the disciples. After the story there follows the second sign of Jesus, the healing of the son of the royal official (4:46-54).

What Kind of Text?

This lively dialogue between Jesus and the Samaritan woman is the only gospel account of a visit of Jesus to Samaria, and it is thought to reflect a special missionary concern by the Johannine church for Samaria. The passage is skilfully written, with plenty of local colour: the Samaritan city, Jacob's well, Mount Gerizim, and good 'stage management'.

Commentary: verse by verse reading

Living Water

vv.5-6 The place-name 'Sychar' is unknown to us from any other document. Possibly it has been misread by an early copyist for Shechem, which was then the main Samaritan city. The two names look similar in Greek.

The book of Genesis records the patriarch Jacob's purchase of land from an individual called Shechem, and his gift of it to his son Joseph. In Genesis 33:18-19 we read: 'Jacob came safely to the city of Shechem, which is in the land of Canaan, on his way from Paddan-aram; he camped before the city. And from the sons of Hamor, Shechem's father, he bought for one hundred pieces of money the plot of land on which he had pitched his tent.' Genesis 48:22 reads: 'Jacob said to Joseph: I now give to you one portion more than to your brothers, the portion that I took from the hand of the Amorites with my sword and with my bow.' There is a clever pun here in the Hebrew. The Hebrew word for 'portion' is *shekem*, which sounds very much like 'Shechem'. Jacob's well is not mentioned in the Old Testament, but its site is still known.

The Samaritans were the descendants of Jews who lived in the northern half of Israel. After the Assyrian invasion and destruction of Samaria in 721 BC, the region was settled by Assyrians. The Samaritans eventually set up their own religious centre on mount Gerizim. They considered only the Pentateuch to be Scripture. In Jesus' day the Samaritans were despised and considered heretical by other Jews.

Jacob's well is thought to be just on the edge of the town of Nablus.

In about 380 AD a church was built on the spot with a baptistry in the crypt. The church was in the form of a cross with the well at its central point. This church, rebuilt in modern times, is now in the care of Greek Orthodox monks. The well is 32 metres deep and visitors can refresh themselves with fresh water from the well.

v.7 Midday is an unusual time at which to come to draw water, in the heat of the day. Some suggest that the woman deliberately came at noon to avoid other women, since she was a notorious sinner, having had five husbands and now another man (verses 17-18). But the evangelist does not give any attention to such a point. It would, in those times, have been considered improper for a teacher to converse alone with a woman, a point that will be alluded to later (verse 27).

v.8 Some state that the 'stage-directions' in this verse are artificial, putting the disciples 'off stage', when they too are tired and thirsty. But things may have happened exactly in this way.

v.9 Especially since the time of the Jewish leader John Hyrcanus (135-104 BC), who conquered Samaria and destroyed the Samaritan temple on Mount Gerizim, relations between the Jews and the Samaritans had been very strained. There were frequent clashes when Jews passed through Samaria, occasionally involving bloodshed. The evangelist appears to be well acquainted with this difficult situation.

That Jews 'do not share things in common with Samaritans' refers to the Jewish presumption of the ritual uncleanness of Samaritan women. Their uncleanness was regarded as transmissible by the vessels and utensils they used. According to that sort of understanding, Jesus would make himself unclean by drinking from a Samaritan woman's water jug.

v.10 Jesus' reply about 'living water' must have been mysterious to the woman, but it serves to raise the conversation to a higher level, from the outward situation, to the inner situation of a person meeting the Saviour.

Is 'the gift of God' Jesus himself, or what he gives? It could be both, since giver and gift merge in Johannine thought. The revealer is himself the revelation. The one who gives the bread of life is himself the bread of life (6:27,35). In Judaism 'the gift of God' was, above all else, the Torah.

'Living water' was also a description of the Torah in Judaism. Here, the 'living water' is the gift conveyed by Jesus. In John 7:37-39 water is explicitly identified by the evangelist as a symbol of the Spirit. Symbols are not static. They can bear different meanings at different times. There is no real contradiction between 4:10 and 7:39 in that it would be the Spirit who would convey to later disciples the life and revelation brought by Jesus.

This water is 'living'. In one sense, that is in obvious contrast to the still water of a well. In another sense, it means 'life-giving', because it confers eternal life.

v.11 'Sir' is *kyrie* in the Greek, and is used again by the woman in verse 15 and verse 19. But it is not easy to see a progression in the woman's understanding from 'Sir', its everyday meaning, to 'Lord', its faith meaning. The woman imagines that the 'living water' of which he speaks comes from a well, though he has no bucket, and the well is deep. As elsewhere, a person's misunderstanding enables Jesus to continue his teaching.

St Augustine comments:

He asks for a drink and promises to give a drink. He longs as one about to receive; he abounds as one about to satisfy. 'If you knew,' he says, 'the gift of God.' The gift of God is the Holy Spirit.

(Tractates on the Gospel of John 15.12)

The Catechism of the Catholic Church reads:

'If you knew the gift of God!' The wonder of prayer is revealed beside the well where we come seeking water: there, Christ comes to meet every human being. It is he who first seeks us and asks us for a drink. Jesus thirsts; his asking arises from the depths of God's desire for us. Whether we realise it or not, prayer is the encounter of God's thirst with ours. God thirsts that we may thirst for him.'

(2560)

The Samaritan Woman by JesusMafa.

v.12 This is an ironical question. Jesus is of course greater than Jacob, as the reader of the gospel knows. The question conveys the woman's suspicion of the greatness of Jesus. The Samaritans held the patriarchs in high honour, especially since the Old Testament prophets were not in their Scriptures.

v.13 The rabbis used the metaphor of 'drinking' for learning from the Torah. There is of course plentiful symbolic usage in the Old Testament of 'thirsting' and 'drinking'.

v.14 The verb 'gushing up' denotes the vitality of the divine forces bestowed, their undiminished vigour and freshness. 'Gushing up to' or 'for' eternal life is an unexpected combination. 'Eternal life' is the goal or purpose of this gift. Even if 'eternal life' has something of a future, eschatological sense here, the gift is given by Jesus in the present.

v.15 The woman continues to misunderstand, asking now for a sort of 'magic' water that will quench all thirst. Jesus' efforts are directed at making her more receptive to revelation, and leading her to believe. The self-revelation of Jesus is the evangelist's principal theme throughout this lively dialogue.

Located between Mt. Gerizim (left) and Mt. Ebal (right) Shechem is preeminent in the biblical record.

Jesus, Prophet and Messiah

vv.16-18 The woman gives an evasive answer, being somewhat economical with the truth. She has had five husbands, and now another partner, as Jesus reminds her. The Samaritans, as much as the Jews, would have regarded such frequent remarriage as dishonourable and illegitimate. Jesus does not condone her matrimonial status. It would appear to be an impediment to her drawing of God's living water, since, if it was of no consequence, it is unclear why he would have mentioned it.

v.19 This is an ironic understatement. Jesus is much more than a prophet, as the reader is aware. The exchange between the two is quite life-like, and some writers comment on the woman's opportune, quick change of subject, steering the conversation away from the embarrassing subject of her marital status to the less personal question of worship.

v.20 The mountain the woman mentions is Mount Gerizim, the site of the Samaritan temple. The 'you' in 'you say' is plural, referring to the Jews and the controversy over Jerusalem and Gerizim.

v.21 When Jesus says 'believe me' it is not so much a call to faith (the usual Johannine meaning), as a call to trust in him. It implies some measure of consolation for the Samaritan people, who have suffered much contempt from the Jews. Jesus teaches a new type of worship, for which the place of offering is unimportant.

v.22 The 'you' is plural, referring to the Samaritans. The 'we' presumably refers to Christians. The statement that 'salvation is from the Jews' is unexpected, given how often 'the Jews' is a negative term in this gospel. But Judaism itself is not rejected, only the unbelieving Jewish leaders of the day. The statement probably derives from early Christian missionary preaching.

v.23 From the perspective of the readers of the gospel, the 'hour' of the saving work of Jesus has been accomplished. They will 'worship in spirit and truth'.

St John Chrysostom comments on the woman's progress:

See how the woman is led step by step to a higher understanding. First, she thought Jesus was some lax Jew who was transgressing the law. Then, when she heard about the living water, she thought it meant material water. Afterwards, she understands it as spoken spiritually and believes that it can take away thirst. However, she does not yet know what it is, only understanding that it was superior to material things.

(Homilies on the Gospel of John 32.1)

Mount Gerizim is spoken of in Deuteronomy 27:12 as the place where the people were ordered by Moses to gather after crossing the Jordan. This mountain could be seen from the Well of Jacob. Some time after the fifth century BC, the Samaritans broke away from the Jerusalem Jews, and built their own temple on Mount Gerizim. It survived until it was destroyed by John Hyrcanus around 112 BC. Even after that, the Samaritans refused to go in pilgrimage to the Jerusalem temple.

The following verse makes clear that 'spirit' means God's spirit, its usual meaning in the Johannine writings, not the human spirit. The statement is not, therefore, about interior, private, non-external worship. 'Truth' in John means the divine reality that is revealed by Jesus, and in which those who believe in him are brought to share.

The reference to the Father 'seeking' demonstrates that the woman must allow God to find her, in responding to Jesus who is speaking to her.

v.24 It is never formally stated by the Old Testament that 'God is spirit', but he reveals himself as such in the Old Testament, by the way his spirit rules over creation and history, giving and restoring life. 'Spirit' denotes what belongs to God and to the heavenly world, in contrast to what is earthly and human.

The human 'must worship in spirit and truth', becoming a different being, transformed by the Spirit. What is decisive is not the place, but the nature of the person who worships, and the way the person worships.

v.25 The woman fails to understand that Jesus is telling her that the present is the hour of fulfilment, and that the fulfilment is in himself. This is another misunderstanding, but at least her religious longings are sincere.

She would not have used the term 'Messiah'. The Samaritans did not expect an anointed king who would sit on the throne of David in Jerusalem. They actually expected a figure called the 'Taheb', 'the one who returns', who would be a political leader and the restorer of true Israel, as well as priest, teacher of the Law and prophet like Moses.

v.26 Jesus reveals to the woman who he is. 'I am he', or 'I am', (*ego eimi* in Greek) reflects the name of God revealed to Moses in Exodus 3:14. This is the climax of the dialogue. The previous themes of living water and worship in spirit and truth now connect with the revelation of who Jesus is. He is the giver of the living water, and the place where the new worship of God takes place.

From the Dogmatic Constitution on the Liturgy (Sacrosanctum Concilium):

By Baptism men and women are implanted in the paschal mystery of Christ; they die with him, are buried with him, and rise with him. They receive the spirit of adoption as sons and daughters 'in which we cry Abba, Father' and thus become true adorers such as the Father seeks. (6)

The Word Lives On

In the Liturgy

The first Eucharistic Prayer, known also as the Roman Canon, contains the following words in the prayer which precedes the consecration:

Bless and approve our offering; make it acceptable to you, an offering in spirit and in truth.

The words 'in spirit and in truth' are obviously taken from John 4.

In the Lectionary

This chapter is an illustration of one woman's journey in faith. From considering Jesus as a prophet she progresses to recognising him as the Messiah, and towards the end of the chapter she spreads the good news by telling her fellow-townspeople about him.

The journey towards faith of the Samaritan woman makes this text very suitable for catechumens as they approach baptism at Easter. At Mass on the Third Sunday of Lent in Year A we hear John 4:5-42, but the same gospel reading may be selected each year thus overriding the gospels for Year B and Year C. The reading from John chapter 4 is of course particularly apposite when catechumens are present at the Sunday Mass.

On the Fourth Sunday of Lent in Year A the story of the man born blind in John chapter 9 is told. It illustrates the gradual enlightenment, both physical and spiritual, of one who was blind from birth. This gospel reading too may override the gospel readings for Year B and Year C.

On the Fifth Sunday of Lent in Year A the story of the raising of Lazarus in John chapter 11 is read. This text not only shows the developing faith of Martha and Mary, but also points to the Resurrection of Christ, the source of new life for all the baptised through the Easter sacraments.

The following 'prayer of exorcism' (a prayer celebrating deliverance from sin and new life in Christ) is taken from the 'Rite of Christian Initiation of Adults' (RCIA) and is used during the First Scrutiny on the Third Sunday of Lent for those preparing for baptism:

God our Father, you sent your Son to be our Saviour: these men and women preparing for baptism thirst for living water as did the Samaritan woman. May the word of the Lord change their lives too, and help them to acknowledge the sins and weaknesses that burden them.

These three great chapters of the Gospel of John serve to intensify the preparation for those approaching baptism at Easter, but also assist all the baptised in their preparation for the renewal of baptismal promises at the Easter Mass. That is why, where it is judged pastorally appropriate, the three-year lectionary cycle can be abandoned on each of these Sundays and the Johannine gospels can be read in Years B and C as well as in Year A.

The Preface for the Third Sunday of Lent, whenever John 4 is the gospel, reads as follows:

When he asked the woman of Samaria for water to drink, Christ had already prepared for her the gift of faith. In his thirst to receive her faith he awakened in her heart the fire of your love.

Whenever John 9 is read as the gospel on the Fourth Sunday of Lent, the Preface includes these words:

He (Jesus) came among us as a man, to lead mankind from darkness into the light of faith.

Whenever John 11 is read as the gospel on the Fifth Sunday of Lent, the Preface reads:

In his love for us all Christ gives us the sacraments to lift us up to everlasting life.

Christ and the Woman from Samaria at Jacob's Well, section of wing panel from the Mompelgarter Altarpiece (panel) by Gerung or Gerou, Matthias (c.1500-68/70).

Live the Word of God

Listen once more to the reading.

What do you hear now?

Suggestions for reflection and prayer

How much progress does the Samaritan woman make on the journey of faith?

Reflect on the words of John Chrysostom about faith given in the margin.

In what ways do Christians still receive 'living water'?

The Samaritan woman is generous and open to the words of Jesus.

❖ Pray for a readiness to discover God's new gifts.

Jesus teaches us the value of worship 'in spirit and truth'.

❖ Pray for a detachment from the outward trappings of worship.

Jesus welcomes dialogue with a woman who does not share the Jewish faith.

❖ Pray for the willingness to discover good things in those of other faith communities.

St John Chrysostom says this about faith:

Everywhere, beloved, we have need of faith. Faith is the mother of all good, the medicine of salvation in order to obtain any real good. Without it, it is impossible to possess any of the great doctrines. Those who try anything without it are like those who venture on the sea without a boat and are drowned because they can barely swim. Similarly, those who try to figure things out before they have learned anything are prone to suffer shipwreck. To ensure that this does not happen to us, let us hold fast to the sacred anchor by which Christ brings over the Samaritan woman.

(Homilies on the Gospel of John 33.1.2)

The Feeding of the Five Thousand

Hear the Word of God

Read John 6:1-13

[1] After this Jesus went to the other side of the Sea of Galilee, also called the Sea of Tiberias. [2] A large crowd kept following him, because they saw the signs that he was doing for the sick. [3] Jesus went up the mountain, and sat down there with his disciples. [4] Now the Passover, the festival of the Jews, was near.

[5] When he looked up and saw a large crowd coming towards him, Jesus said to Philip, 'Where are we to buy bread for these people to eat?' [6] He said this to test him, for he himself knew what he was going to do. [7] Philip answered him, 'Six months' wages would not buy enough bread for each of them to get a little.'

[8] One of his disciples, Andrew, Simon Peter's brother, said to him, 'There is a boy here who has five barley loaves and two fish. But what are they among so many people?' [10] Jesus said, 'Make the people sit down.' Now there was a great deal of grass in the place; so they sat down, about five thousand in all. [11] Then Jesus took the loaves, and when he had given thanks, he distributed them to those who were seated; so also the fish, as much as they wanted. [12] When they were satisfied, he told his disciples, 'Gather up the fragments left over, so that nothing may be lost.'

[13] So they gathered them up, and from the fragments of the five barley loaves, left by those who had eaten, they filled twelve baskets.

Opposite: The Feeding of the Five Thousand by Joachim Patenier(1487-1524).

Understand the Word of God

This session will explore:

- ❖ the account of this sign in John
- ❖ similarities and differences in the synoptic accounts
- ❖ connections with the Last Supper

Setting in the Gospel

Following Jesus' visit to Samaria in chapter 4, in chapter 5 he has been in Jerusalem, where he healed the man who had been ill for thirty-eight years at the Pool of Bethzatha. This was the third of the seven signs. Now Jesus is back in Galilee. Unlike in the synoptic gospels, in John the ministry of Jesus goes back and forth between Galilee and Jerusalem. It is clear from John's gospel that Jesus paid several visits to Jerusalem during his ministry.

The Feeding of the Five Thousand, 1479 by Alexander Bening, (d. 1519)

What Kind of Text?

For John this is the fourth of the seven signs of the ministry of Jesus. It is recounted also in the synoptic gospels, in Mark 6:30-44 and the parallels in Matthew 14:13-21 and Luke 9:10-17. This is the only miracle from the public ministry recounted in all four gospels. John's version is notably different from the other accounts. The wording is very different. Interestingly, in Matthew and Mark, as also in John, this narrative is immediately followed by the account of Jesus' night-time walking on the waters.

Mark 8:1-9 and Matthew 15:29-39 give an account of a second miraculous feeding, this time of four thousand people with seven loaves and a few fishes. Most take it to be a variant or duplicate of the Feeding of the Five Thousand that existed in some pre-gospel traditions. Luke omits the Feeding of the Four Thousand from his gospel.

Commentary: verse by verse reading

Jesus and the Crowd

v.1 'After this' gives a very loose connection with what precedes, as often is the case in this gospel. And there is a difficulty about the sequence of events. In chapter 5 Jesus is in Jerusalem; now he is crossing the Sea of Galilee from one side to the other. We have no idea or indication from which side of the lake Jesus travelled, or to which side he went, and it is pointless to speculate.

In time Jews began to live in Tiberias and it became the largest town of Galilee. In the third century AD a great rabbinic school was founded at Tiberias. The scholars took forward the study of the Mishnah, the second century compilation of law, and by about 400 AD produced the Gemara, a second body of laws. Mishnah and Gemara together make up the Talmud. Due to Christian pressure the school of Tiberias began to collapse in the fifth century. Visitors can still visit what is considered the site of the school in Tiberias.

The biblical languages use the same words for a 'lake' and a 'sea'. The Sea of Galilee is, of course, an inland, freshwater lake. It has a variety of different names in biblical tradition. Here it is also given its most recent new name, 'the Sea of Tiberias'. In Jesus' time the town of Tiberias was newly completed, having been founded in 18 AD by Herod Antipas to replace Sepphoris as his main residence. It was only after the time of Jesus that the town-name, Tiberias, was used of the lake. Observant Jews would not live in or go near Tiberias. When its construction started, its builders unearthed an ancient burial site, making it an unclean place for Jewish people who could be ritually contaminated by contact with corpses. For this reason Herod Antipas was forced to recruit soldiers, non-Jews, freed slaves and landless people to populate his new city.

v.2 If Jesus travelled by boat (as we assume), it is not clear whether the people followed him by boat or on foot. Mark's account (6:33) speaks of many people running on foot from all the towns to reach their destination before Jesus. These details are not in John's account.

St John Chrysostom comments on the evangelist's selection of the signs of Jesus:

Observe, in a whole year, the evangelist has told us of no miracles of Christ, except of his healing of the paralytic and the nobleman's son. His purpose was not to enumerate them all, which would have been impossible, but to record the great principal acts of our Lord.

(Homilies on the Gospel of John 42.1)

The reference to 'the signs that he was doing for the sick' suggests that Jesus has performed a number of healings in Galilee. In fact, the gospel has so far recounted only two healings by Jesus: the royal official's son in Galilee in 4:46-51 and the sick man at the Pool of Bethzatha in Jerusalem in chapter 5. The signs that are narrated in John are of course a selection of all that Jesus did, as 20:30 explains.

v.3 In John's narrative the people have not yet arrived. Only John mentions Jesus going up the mountain. Jesus sits down presumably in order to teach, since sitting was the usual position for teaching. 'His disciples' are probably to be understood as the Twelve, as they are in Mark 6:30. John very rarely uses the term 'the twelve', and never uses the term 'apostle'.

v.4 It is probably significant to state that it was Passover in view of the Passover and Exodus themes that will follow in Jesus' teaching later in the chapter, which is commonly referred to as 'the Bread of Life discourse'. This is the second of three Passovers that are mentioned in John, the others being found in 2:13 and 11:55. The three Passovers gave rise to the idea that the public ministry of Jesus had to have lasted for three years. Like 'the mountain' Passover is not mentioned in the accounts in the other gospels. It does seem somewhat unnecessary for the writer to inform his readers that the Passover was 'the feast of the Jews', but this may be a catechetical explanation for those unfamiliar with Jewish practices.

v.5 At this point in John's account the crowd arrives. In Mark they arrived on foot ahead of Jesus and the disciples. Other details of Mark that are not in John include Jesus having compassion on them, because they were like sheep without a shepherd, his teaching them many things by which time it had grown late, and the disciples asking him to send the people away to buy food.

More from St John Chrysostom:

Jesus went up to the mountain as a lesson to us to retire from the tumult and confusion of the world. For solitude is appropriate for the study of wisdom.

(Homilies on the Gospel of John 42.1)

The three Passovers in John's gospel:

2:13 The Passover of the Jews was near, and Jesus went up to Jerusalem.

6:4 Now the Passover, the festival of the Jews, was near.

11:55 Now the Passover of the Jews was near, and many went up from the country to Jerusalem before the Passover to purify themselves.

Jesus multiplies the Loaves by JesusMafa.

Texts pointing to Jesus' superior knowledge:

2:24-25 But Jesus on his part would not entrust himself to them, because he knew all people and needed no one to testify about anyone; for he himself knew what was in everyone.

5:6 When Jesus saw him lying there and knew that he had been there a long time, he said to him: Do you want to be made well?

6:64 For Jesus knew from the first who were the ones that did not believe, and who was the one that would betray him.

In John there is no mention of Jesus teaching the crowd or of the late hour. Jesus simply takes the initiative about giving them food by asking Philip: 'Where are we to buy bread for these people to eat?' Philip is not mentioned in the synoptic accounts.

v.6 This explanation by the evangelist makes clear to the reader that Jesus was not asking the question because he did not know what to do about the situation. Quite the opposite: 'He himself knew what he would do.' This is another reference to the superior knowledge of Jesus that is expressed various times in the Fourth Gospel.

The word 'test' can also mean 'tempt', but 'testing', rather than 'tempting to evil', is the sense here. Jesus has presumably now come down from the mountain. As elsewhere the evangelist is not concerned with full narrative detail, such as we might have in a modern novel.

v.7 Six months' wages is literally two hundred denarii. From Matthew's parable of the labourers in the vineyard we learn that a denarius was one day's pay. In Mark 6:37 there appears to be an interesting agreement in detail, when the disciples say to Jesus: 'Are we to go and buy two hundred denarii worth of bread, and give it to them to eat?' But the import is different. In Mark's question it seems that that amount of bread would be sufficient to feed them. In John it is not. Again John has not drawn on the synoptic accounts for anything in his gospel, and those agreements that there are must go back to the oral traditions about Jesus.

The Working of the Sign

vv.8-9 Andrew had been identified at 1:40 as Simon Peter's brother, and the identification is repeated here. Like Philip he is not mentioned in the synoptic accounts. He will appear again at 12:22, where he and Philip, again associated, tell Jesus of the Greeks at the Passover festival who wish to see him.

The mention of a boy, and of barley bread, neither of which occur in the synoptic accounts, suggests background for John's narrative in Elisha's miracle in the second Book of Kings.

The 2 Kings text speaks of Elisha's 'servant', but this may well have become 'lad' or 'boy' in the story-telling tradition. The evangelist's mention of 'barley' in verses 9 and 13 may be because it was used by the Johannine church for its Eucharist. Since barley bread was often eaten by the poor, it may indicate that it was a poor community. It may be that it was more easily obtained by them.

In this gospel, Jesus will again give bread and fish to his disciples (though not to a crowd), and again by the Lake of Galilee, in his resurrection appearance at 21:13.

v.10 The plentiful grass ties in with the springtide Passover setting. Mark 6:39 speaks of 'green grass'. The original Greek text translated as 'they sat down, about five thousand in all' is actually 'the men sat down, in number about five thousand'. Mark 6:44 also speaks of five thousand men, but Matthew 14:21 adds 'besides women and children'. This suggests that more than five thousand people were fed.

v.11 The actions of Jesus are important: 'he took ... he gave thanks ... he distributed.' Giving thanks (in Greek *eucharistesas*) is probably deliberately used to evoke the Eucharist. 'Distributed' is the Greek verb for 'give' with a preposition, resulting in 'he gave out'. Is this another Eucharistic allusion?

In the Gospel of Mark Jesus' actions are somewhat different: 'he looked up to heaven ... he blessed ... he broke the loaves ... he gave

2 Kings 4:42-44

A man came from Baal-shalishah, bringing food from the first fruits to the man of God: twenty loaves of barley and fresh ears of grain in his sack. Elisha said: Give it to the people and let them eat. But his servant said: How can I set this before a hundred people? So he repeated: Give it to the people and let them eat, for thus says the Lord: They shall eat and have some left. He set it before them, they ate, and had some left, according to the word of the Lord.

them to the disciples.' There is no significant difference between John's 'he gave thanks' and Mark's 'he blessed'. Both probably represent the same Hebrew verb *barak*, which means 'to bless'.

Mark's wording for the feeding of the five thousand is very close to the wording of his Last Supper account: 'he took the bread ... he blessed it... he broke it... he gave it to them ... Then he took a cup ... gave thanks .... gave it to them ...' (14:22-23).

There is no doubt that Jesus' actions in the different gospel accounts of the feeding of the five thousand evoke his actions at the Last Supper. Why else would Mark describe him as 'breaking' the bread for feeding the five thousand? And no such actions over the fish are mentioned in any of the accounts.

Does 'he distributed them' mean Jesus himself did this? More likely, given the size of the crowd, it was the disciples who distributed the loaves, as Mark 6:41 states: 'He gave the loaves to his disciples to set before the people.' John preserves a hint of the Twelve being involved in the distribution in his statement in verse 13 that twelve baskets were filled with the fragments left over. 'To those who were seated', or 'were reclining', is significant since people reclined to eat the Passover.

v.12 All the gospel accounts record the people's satisfaction. But the instruction in John to gather up the fragments does not occur in the synoptic accounts. It is not a 'keep Galilee tidy' campaign by Jesus. It is thought to be in the text to teach care for the eucharistic elements, as well as for the individuals who compose the eucharistic body.

There are other relevant texts that use the same verb 'lose', which is used here of the fragments of the loaves, to refer to people. In 6:39 we read: 'This is the will of him who sent me, that I should lose nothing of all that he has given me, but raise it up on the last day.' In 17:12 we read: 'I protected them in your name that you have given me, and not one of them was lost, except the one destined to be lost, so that the scripture might be fulfilled.'

St Augustine writes:

He created as God creates. For, just as he multiplies the produce of the fields from a few grains, from that same source of power he multiplied in his hands the five loaves. There was power, indeed, in the hands of Christ. And those five loaves were like seeds, not indeed committed to the earth, but multiplied by him who made the earth.

(Tractates on the Gospel of John 24.1)

The 'Didache', or 'Teaching of the Twelve Apostles' was written not long after the Fourth Gospel. It uses several of the same words:

Concerning the fragmented bread ... we give thanks to you, our Father ... As this fragmented bread was scattered on the mountains, but was then gathered up and became one, so may the Church be gathered up from the four corners of the earth into your Kingdom. (9:4)

v.13 The synoptic accounts agree about twelve baskets being filled with the fragments. There have already been many possible pointers to the Eucharist in John's account. The Passover setting in verse 4 suggests the Christian Eucharist. Also 'Jesus took ... and gave thanks and gave out' in verse 11, and the reference to 'those reclining' in the same verse. Gathering up the fragments in verses 12-13, and the fact that there is no reference to gathering up what is left over from the fishes, are further pointers.

In the opinion of many scholars, there are only two specifically sacramental passages in John's gospel. These are John 3:5, with its reference to being born 'of water and the Spirit', and 6:51-58, our next text. In addition, it seems that John's account of the feeding of the five thousand has unmistakable sacramental overtones. This is what makes this sign-story particularly rich and relevant.

St Cyril of Alexandria, bishop and great theologian in the early part of the fifth century, provides a further comment on the meaning of the sign:

Initially the disciples were reluctant to feed the hungry, but, seeing this, the Saviour gave to them in abundance from the fragments. This teaches us as well, that by expending a little for the glory of God we shall receive richer grace according to the saying of Christ, 'a good measure, pressed down, shaken together, running over, will be put into your lap'. Therefore, we must not be slothful regarding the communion of love toward our brothers and sisters, but rather put away from us, as far as possible, the cowardice and fear that lead to inhospitality.

(Commentary on the Gospel of John 3.4)

The Word Lives On

Our detailed look at the text of the Feeding of the Five Thousand and our awareness of the parallel accounts in the other gospels have shown how important this text is.

Hearing any of the Eucharistic Prayers we use at Mass will immediately recall parts of the story we have just examined.

In the Lectionary

The abundance of parallel accounts of the feeding of multitudes means that there is much to choose from when a particular feast suggests such a gospel reading. The three gospel readings provided for the Solemnity of the Body and Blood of Christ (Corpus Christi) in the three year cycle are the conclusion of the Bread of Life discourse in John chapter 6, Mark's account of the Last Supper, and Luke's account of the Feeding of the Five Thousand.

Nevertheless, John chapter 6 as a whole is not neglected. It has a particularly interesting place in the lectionary. The Sundays in Ordinary Time generally are apportioned readings from the synoptic gospels in the sequence Matthew, Mark, Luke. Due to the shortness of the Gospel of Mark, John chapter 6 is inserted during the Year of Mark from the 17th to the 21st Sunday. It is inserted precisely at the point in Mark's gospel where the first feeding of the multitude would have been read.

John chapter 6 is a particularly long chapter, comprising seventy-one verses. Since it is spread over five Sundays, a rich opportunity is provided for exploring the various dimensions of the text and preaching on the Eucharist.

Live the Word of God

Listen once more to the reading.

What do you hear now?
Suggestions for reflection and prayer

What does this sign in John's gospel point to?

Reflect on the passage from Pope John Paul II given in the margin.

In what ways does this text recall the Eucharist?

The first concern of Jesus is for the physical needs of the people.
❖ Pray for those who endeavour to feed the hungry in our own society and across the world.

Philip and Andrew seem unaware of the power of Jesus to provide for those in need.
❖ Pray for a deeper faith that with good will the problems of need can be addressed.

In the Eucharist the giver and the gift are one.
❖ Pray for generosity of heart as disciples of Christ.

Pope John Paul II wrote in his encyclical on the Eucharist:

In repeating what Christ did at the Last Supper in obedience to his command: Do this in memory of me, we also accept Mary's invitation to obey him without hesitation: Do whatever he tells you (John 2:5). With the same maternal concern which she showed at the wedding feast of Cana, Mary seems to say to us: Do not waver; trust in the words of my Son. If he was able to change water into wine, he can also turn bread and wine into his body and blood, and through this mystery bestow on believers the living memorial of his Passover, thus becoming the 'bread of life'.

(Ecclesia de Eucharistia 54)

Mosaic at the Church of the Multiplication of the Loaves, Galilee (5th century).

The Discourse on the Bread of Life

Hear the Word of God

Read John 6:51-59

[51] Jesus said: 'I am the living bread that came down from heaven. Whoever eats of this bread will live for ever; and the bread that I will give for the life of the world is my flesh.'

[52] The Jews then disputed among themselves, saying, 'How can this man give us his flesh to eat?'

[53] So Jesus said to them, 'Very truly I tell you, unless you eat the flesh of the Son of Man and drink his blood, you have no life in you. [54] Those who eat my flesh and drink my blood have eternal life, and I will raise them up on the last day; [55] for my flesh is true food and my blood is true drink. [56] Those who eat my flesh and drink my blood abide in me, and I in them. [57] Just as the living Father sent me, and I live because of the Father, so whoever eats me will live because of me. [58] This is the bread that came down from heaven, not like that which your ancestors ate, and they died. But the one who eats this bread will live for ever.'

[59] He said these things while he was teaching in the synagogue at Capernaum.

Opposite: Scenes from the life of Jesus Christ: Last supper, 15th century.

Understand the Word of God

This session will explore:

❖ the Bread of Life discourse

❖ what it means to eat the flesh of Jesus

❖ the bread eaten by the ancestors

Setting in the Gospel

The feeding of the five thousand in 6:1-13 is followed by the night-time walking on the waters in 6:16-21. On the following day Jesus again meets the crowd and, after their unexpected request to him for a sign in 6:30, he starts speaking to them about the Bread of Life.

Our text, which concludes the discourse of Jesus in chapter 6, is followed by an account of the reaction of the disciples to Jesus' 'difficult teaching' (verse 60).

What Kind of Text?

The first main section of the Bread of Life discourse, in John 6:32-50, is about the teaching or revealing of Jesus to be the Bread of Life that feeds people. In those verses the response to Jesus is belief, not eating. In verse 35 we read: 'Whoever comes to me will never be hungry, whoever believes in me will never be thirsty.' Verse 36 continues with the theme of belief: 'you have seen me and yet do not believe.' In verse 40 Jesus says that 'all who see the Son and believe in him may have eternal life'. In verse 47 he emphasises the point again: 'Whoever believes has eternal life.'

It is only in verse 50 that 'eating' is mentioned, and 'drinking' in verse 53. Verses 51-58 are eucharistic: they concern the flesh and blood of Jesus, and eating and drinking it.

It seems therefore that in John chapter 6 the evangelist has given us two versions or traditions of the Bread of Life discourse. The first tradition is 'sapiential', concerned with wisdom and the teaching of Jesus. The second tradition is sacramental.

There is some parallelism between the two traditions. Both include an interruption, contradiction or challenge by the audience. In verse 41 the objection of the Jews concerns knowing where Jesus came from, and his claims that he comes from heaven. In verse 52 the objection is: 'How can this man give us his flesh to eat?' In addition, both traditions speak of the ancestors eating manna (in verses 49 and 58).

There is some difference of opinion as to where exactly the second tradition begins. The New Revised Standard Version Bible begins the new paragraph at verse 52. We will begin at verse 51, because it is in this verse that we find the first mention of the 'flesh' of Jesus.

Commentary: verse by verse reading

v.51 'Living bread' here means the same as 'bread of life' in verse 35. The person who eats this bread will 'live for ever'. In verse 50 we heard that the person 'will not die' and in verse 37 that 'I will never drive the person away'. Both these phrases are reminiscent of the Book of Genesis and the story of the forbidden fruit and the expulsion from the garden of Eden. The man and woman are told by the serpent that they will 'not die' (*Genesis* 3:4) and at the end of the chapter they are driven away from the garden by God (*Genesis* 3:24). Are these deliberate allusions to the Book of Genesis? The emphasis is that those who eat the bread of life will truly not die and that they will never be driven away by God.

We now have the first reference to the 'flesh' (Greek *sarx*) of Jesus. Earlier, in verses 32-50, what we have called the 'sapiential' tradition, it was Jesus' revelation, his teaching, that was presented as the means to eternal life. Now it is eating his 'flesh' that leads to life.

Although biblical Hebrew, and the Aramaic spoken by Jesus, had a word for 'corpse', there was no word for the 'body' of a living person. It is probable that at the Last Supper Jesus spoke Aramaic and said: 'This is my flesh' and 'This is my blood.' This is reflected in the use here in the Greek of John's gospel of the word *sarx*. This is different from the Last Supper accounts in the synoptic gospels, in which Jesus says: 'This is my body (Greek *soma*)' and 'This is the cup of my blood.' In the words found in the synoptic gospels there is less possibility of the awkward misunderstanding that eating the Eucharist is some kind of cannibalistic rite.

Unlike in the translation from the New Revised Standard Version Bible, the statement should possibly be read as 'the bread that I will give is my flesh for the life of the world', with the phrase 'for the life of the world' at the end, after 'my flesh'. This would be a Johannine equivalent of Jesus' statement in the synoptic accounts: 'This is my body which is given for you.' The 'for' is sacrificial and concerns the self-giving of Jesus for God's people.

v.52 Disputing, quarrelling, or wrangling by the Jews occurs again. They were heard 'complaining' earlier in verse 41. The Old Testament spoke of the people both complaining to Moses about the lack of food, and quarrelling with him about the lack of water.

The Jews are disputing 'among themselves'. Nevertheless, it constitutes rebellion against God through unbelief. They misunderstand, taking Jesus' words in a materialistic sense, as often happens in the misunderstandings in John's gospel. Another good example is found in John 4:15 when the Samaritan woman says: 'Sir, give me this water, so that I may never be thirsty or have to keep coming here to draw water.'

Some would explain the Jews' misunderstanding as due to the abhorrent thought of consuming a person's blood in eating living, human flesh, an action strongly forbidden to the Jews, but this is not explicitly stated by the text.

Exodus 16:2 The whole congregation of the Israelites complained against Moses and Aaron in the wilderness.

Exodus 17:2-3 The people quarrelled with Moses, and said, 'Give us water to drink.' Moses said to them, 'Why do you quarrel with me? Why do you test the Lord?' But the people thirsted there for water; and the people complained against Moses.

Numbers 20:3 The people quarrelled with Moses and said, 'Would that we had died when our kindred died before the Lord!'

Numbers 20:13 These are the waters of Meribah, where the people of Israel quarrelled with the Lord, and by which he showed his holiness.

v.53 The 'very truly' in our translation is actually 'Amen, Amen'. It indicates a solemn assurance in what Jesus is saying. When Jesus says, 'you have no life in you,' the reference is to eternal life as always in John.

Jesus' response seems to be deliberately sharp, taking back none of his words, but in effect increasing the potential offence as he speaks also of 'drinking his blood'. 'Blood' is mentioned for the first time. The 'unless' is a strong condition, stronger than it was in verse 51, where it was simply 'whoever eats of this bread will live for ever'.

Why is so sharp a wording used, one which makes reception of the Eucharist essential for having life? Some suggest that certain groups with unorthodox Christian beliefs, known as Gnostics and Docetists, are targeted here. Both the Gnostics, who considered themselves to have a special 'knowledge', and the Docetists tended to deny the reality of the Son of God becoming human and of the death of the Son of God, saying that both were just an appearance. By extension they rejected the presence of Christ in the Eucharist, and reception of the Eucharist.

v.54 Reference to 'the last day' occurs frequently in the discourse like a refrain. In verse 39 Jesus said: 'This is the will of him who sent me, that I should lose nothing of all that he has given me, but raise it up on the last day.' A similar statement is found in verse 40 and again in verse 44. Reference to the last day is known technically as 'future eschatology'. Eschatology is everything which relates to the 'last things'. The last day here is the day at the end of time.

This differs from the evangelist's usual and characteristic eschatology, which is technically referred to as 'realised'. In other words, eschatology is already among us. For this evangelist the gifts of eternal life are already possessed now. The evangelist is perhaps using this 'future eschatology' in order once again to challenge the Gnostics, who denied a future resurrection.

The Greek word used here for 'to eat', (*trogo*), found also in verses 56, 57 and 58, is not the usual word (*esthio / ephagon*), but one which means literally to 'chew' or 'munch'. This is in no way a disrespectful term, and it is used later in John 13:18 in the narrative of the Last Supper, when Jesus quotes from Psalm 41 that 'the one who ate (or chewed) my bread has lifted his heel against me'. It may be used simply as an alternative for the usual 'to eat', which occurs frequently elsewhere in chapter 6.

Some ask whether a deliberate realism of 'chewing' or 'munching' is intended, perhaps to prevent any dilution of what is being taught. This is real eating, not simply an appearance, as the Docetists taught. The word may have been chosen to distinguish the real eating envisaged in verses 51-58 from the symbolic 'eating' of the bread from heaven in verses 32-50.

v.55 When Jesus refers to 'true' food and 'true' drink, he uses the Greek word *alethes*. The New Revised Standard Version Bible has 'true', which is preferable to the Jerusalem Bible translation 'real'. It is 'true' in the sense of 'reliable'. It fulfils what was promised. It brings eternal life.

v.56 The terms 'flesh' and 'blood' undoubtedly come from the eucharistic language of the Johannine community. It is notable that the elements of bread and wine are never mentioned here.

The verb 'abide', 'dwell' or 'remain' speaks of the mutual indwelling of Jesus in the disciples, and the disciples in Jesus. An intimate relationship with Jesus is brought about, an enduring union with the divine bearer of life, bringing the recipient into the sphere of God's life, which is the very purpose of the eating and drinking. The sacramental union becomes a personal union.

This evangelist speaks repeatedly of what is true and reliable, using both alethes and alethinos, which has a closely similar meaning:

1:9 The true light, which enlightens everyone, was coming into the world.

5:32 There is another who testifies on my behalf, and I know that his testimony to me is true.

7:28 The one who sent me is true, and you do not know him.

15:1 I am the true vine.

Some have asked whether there is eucharistic symbolism in John 15:4-5 too:

Abide in me as I abide in you. Just as the branch cannot bear fruit by itself unless it abides in the vine, neither can you unless you abide in me. I am the vine, you are the branches. Those who abide in me and I in them bear much fruit, because apart from me you can do nothing.

Detail of Last Supper Tapestry at Palazzo del Quirinale, Rome.

This is the first occurrence in the gospel of this 'formula of reciprocal union', that the believer abides in Jesus and Jesus in the believer. In human relationships, there could be no such mutual indwelling without loss of personality.

v.57 In verse 51 Jesus had referred to 'this bread', and in verse 54 to 'my flesh'. Here in verse 57 in a more personal expression Jesus says 'whoever eats me'. Those who eat of Jesus are taken up into his life which comes from God.

v.58 'This is the bread that came down from heaven.' 'This' refers to the Son. There is no mention now of 'flesh' and 'blood'. The Son is the bread come down from heaven, who gives life. We have returned to the ideas in verses 35-51, about coming down from heaven. The bread which their ancestors ate is of course the manna, which had previously been referred to in verse 49.

In his first letter to the Corinthians St Paul writes as follows about the journey of Moses and the Israelites through the desert: 'I do not want you to be unaware, brothers and sisters, that our ancestors were all under the cloud, and all passed through the sea, and all were baptised into Moses in the cloud and in the sea, and all ate the same spiritual food, and all drank the same spiritual drink. For they drank from the spiritual rock that followed them, and the rock was Christ.' (1 *Corinthians* 10:1-4)

Paul considers that the Old Testament realities of the manna and the water from the rock, which are found in the books of Exodus and of Numbers, are a preparation for Christ. They are considered to be what are known as 'types' of Christ. These 'types' are things in the Old Testament which foreshadow things in the New. The 'spiritual food and drink' of the Old Testament are seen as 'types' of Christ. John's gospel uses the same early Christian approach of finding types of Christ and of the Eucharist in the Old Testament.

v.59 This verse, which closes the account with reference to Jesus teaching in the synagogue at Capernaum, is quite a surprise. We had no previous notion that Jesus was teaching in a formal setting. Biblical archaeologists remind us that 'synagogue' is a Greek word meaning 'gathering', 'assembly', and that for first century Palestine we should not always imagine a synagogue building. Many of the community assemblies in the villages would have taken place in people's homes, or out of doors.

Synagogue teaching implies teaching on the sabbath, when travel would have been difficult. What should we make therefore of the moving around of Jesus, the disciples and the crowd earlier in the chapter, in verses 16-24? Some scholars believe that the putting together of the various elements in this chapter of the gospel is the evangelist's own creative work, in which case the references to travel would not necessarily be related to travel on the sabbath.

In fact, some have questioned how this eucharistic section of the Bread of Life discourse could have been historically spoken by Jesus, and understood by anybody at all, since it comes before his giving bread and wine as his body and blood at the Last Supper. The institution of the Eucharist is not found in the Last Supper account in the Fourth Gospel. These verses make up a Johannine equivalent for the accounts of the Last Supper in the synoptic gospels. They may in fact derive from the liturgy and preaching of the Johannine church, and are modelled on the 'sapiential' part of the discourse in verses 35-50.

From the Catechism of the Catholic Church:

The three synoptic gospels and St Paul have handed on to us the account of the institution of the Eucharist; St John, for his part, reports the words of Jesus in the synagogue of Capernaum that prepare for the institution of the Eucharist: Christ calls himself the bread of life, come down from heaven. (1338)

Synagogue at Capernaum.

The Word Lives On

In the Lectionary

This part of John chapter 6 is read as the gospel reading on the Solemnity of the Body and Blood of Christ in Year A.

John chapter 6 is read on five Sundays of Ordinary Time during Year B. From the 17th to the 21st Sunday the whole of the chapter is heard at Sunday Mass. The shortness of the Gospel of Mark allows for this insertion and John 6 is read when we reach the point in Mark at which the first account of the feeding of a multitude comes. This perhaps rather contrived insertion of such a lengthy chapter of the Fourth Gospel in fact provides a rich opportunity for reflection and preaching on the meaning of the miracle and its relevance to the Eucharist.

The whole of the chapter is also read during the Easter period, from the Friday of the 2nd week to the Saturday of the 3rd week. The Easter season offers many opportunities to reflect on the deeper significance of Jesus, and it is for this reason that the richly theological Gospel of John is read on all the week-days of the Easter period, as well as many of the Sundays.

Live the Word of God

Listen once more to the reading

What do you hear now?

Suggestions for reflection and prayer

What does eating the flesh and drinking the blood of the Lord mean in your life?

Reflect on the passage from Pope Benedict XVI given in the margin.

How significant is the idea of 'life' in this passage?

The self-giving of Jesus invites our own self-giving.

❖ Pray for generosity in imitating the one we receive in the Eucharist.

The disciples will describe this teaching of Jesus as 'difficult'.

❖ Pray for an acceptance of those elements of our faith which are beyond our full comprehension.

This passage prepares us for the death of Jesus.

❖ Pray that we will not isolate the Eucharist from the problems of daily life.

Pope Benedict XVI writes in Sacramentum Caritatis:

'The bread I will give is my flesh, for the life of the world.' In these words the Lord reveals the true meaning of the gift of his life for all people. These words also reveal his deep compassion for every man and woman. The gospels frequently speak of Jesus' feelings towards others, especially the suffering and sinners. Through a profoundly human sensibility he expresses God's saving will for all people – that they may have true life. Each celebration of the Eucharist makes sacramentally present the gift that the crucified Lord made of his life, for us and for the whole world. In the Eucharist Jesus also makes us witnesses of God's compassion towards all our brothers and sisters. (88)

Jesus as Sheepgate
and Shepherd

Hear the Word of God

Read John 10:1-18

[1] (Jesus said) 'Very truly, I tell you, anyone who does not enter the sheepfold by the gate, but climbs in by another way, is a thief and bandit. [2] The one who enters by the gate is the shepherd of the sheep. [3] The gatekeeper opens the gate for him, and the sheep hear his voice. He calls his own sheep by name and leads them out.

[4] 'When he has brought out all his own, he goes ahead of them, and the sheep follow him because they know his voice. [5] They will not follow a stranger, but they will run from him because they do not know the voice of strangers.' [6] Jesus used this figure of speech with them, but they did not understand what he was saying to them.

[7] So again Jesus said to them, 'Very truly, I tell you, I am the gate for the sheep. [8]

'All who came before me are thieves and bandits; but the sheep did not listen to them. [9] I am the gate. Whoever enters by me will be saved, and will come in and go out and find pasture. [10] The thief comes only to steal and kill and destroy. I came that they may have life, and have it abundantly.

[11] 'I am the good shepherd. The good shepherd lays down his life for the sheep.

[12] 'The hired hand, who is not the shepherd and does not own the sheep, sees the wolf coming and leaves the sheep and runs away - and the wolf snatches them and scatters them. [13] The hired hand runs away because a hired hand does not care for the sheep. [14] I am the good shepherd. I know my own and my own know me, [15] just as the Father knows me and I know the Father. And I lay down my life for the sheep. [16] I have other sheep that do not belong to this fold. I must bring them also, and they will listen to my voice. So there will be one flock, one shepherd. [17] For this reason the Father loves me, because I lay down my life in order to take it up again. [18] No one takes it from me, but I lay it down of my own accord. I have power to lay it down, and I have power to take it up again. I have received this command from my Father.'

Opposite: The Good Shepherd, lunette from above the church entrance (mosaic) by Paleo-Christian, (5th century).

Understand the Word of God

This session will explore:

- ❖ the image of the gate
- ❖ the image of the shepherd
- ❖ Jesus laying down his life and taking it up again

Setting in the Gospel

In chapter 9 Jesus is in Jerusalem where he heals the man born blind. The discourse of chapter 10 begins quite abruptly, without any sort of introduction or transition from the narrative and conversation of chapter 9. After this speech of Jesus, in verses 19-21, there is division among those who heard him, and a reference back to the healing of the blind man in chapter 9.

What Kind of Text?

This parable-type discourse of Jesus includes two different basic 'I am' (*ego eimi*) statements of Jesus, each stated twice: 'I am the gate (of the sheep)' in verses 7 and 9, and 'I am the shepherd' in verses 11 and 14. In some translations, the Greek word *thura* translated here as 'gate' is translated as 'door'. The enemy is described in various ways: as thief and bandit in verses 1, 8 and 10, as a stranger in verse 5, as a wolf in verse 12, and as a hired hand in verses 12-13.

St John Chrysostom writes in a homily on this chapter:

When our Lord calls himself the door, we should not be surprised. According to the office that he bears, he is in one place the shepherd, in another the door. In that he introduces us to the Father, he is the door; in that he takes care of us, he is the shepherd.

(Homilies on the Gospel of John 59.3)

The Good Shepherd by Philippe de Champaigne, (1602-74).

Commentary: verse by verse reading

The Sheepgate

v.1 Jesus begins with the words 'Very truly', which are in Greek *Amen, amen*. This solemn introduction is used twenty-five times by Jesus in this gospel in order to stress the importance of what follows. Other examples are found in 1:51 and 6:53, and in verse 7 of this chapter.

Jesus talks about entering the 'sheepfold'. 'Sheepfold' is literally the 'court' or 'courtyard of the sheep', usually the enclosed courtyard of a house where the sheep were kept safe. Our English word 'fold' means 'enclosure' or 'pen'.

Anyone entering in an unauthorised way is a 'thief and bandit'. 'Bandit' will be used later in this gospel of Barabbas at John 18:40. 'Thief' and 'bandit' are probably two words for the same thing. A distinction between a thief, who comes on the quiet, and a bandit, who resorts to violence, is not necessarily in mind.

Numbers 27:16-17 says this of Joshua:

Let the Lord appoint someone over the congregation, who shall go out before them and come in before them, who shall lead them out and bring them in, so that the congregation of the Lord may not be like sheep without a shepherd.

This text is evidently in mind in Mark 6:34:

As Jesus went shore, he saw a great crowd; and he had compassion for them, because they were like sheep without a shepherd; and he began to teach them many things.

v.2 Jesus speaks of the shepherd who enters by the gate. We imagine that he is speaking of himself as the shepherd, though in verse 7 he will describe himself as 'the gate of the sheep'. The confusion to the reader is caused by the fact of different pronouncements of Jesus being woven together. Verses 1-2 have set up deliberate opposites. The thief and the bandit are contrasted with the shepherd. Coming in 'by another way' is contrasted with coming in 'by the gate'.

v.3 The reference to the 'gatekeeper' here is unique and no more mention of him is found in this chapter. The sheep follow the voice of Jesus, the shepherd. There seems to be some exaggeration in the statement that he calls his own sheep by name. While a shepherd could give names to some of his flock, like 'long-ears' or 'white-nose', it is hard to believe that he could supply names for all of them. Sheep-farmers say that sheep do not actually respond to the calling of a name. Even if the picture is unrealistic, it does portray the shepherd's loving familiarity with his sheep, and their relationship.

Palestinian shepherds go before their sheep, not following from behind with dogs, as with English, Australian, and New Zealander shepherds. It is clear that the shepherding of God's people involves leading.

v.4 The verbs 'knowing' and 'following' have deeper significance for the readers of this gospel. 'Knowing' means knowing Jesus as the one who reveals God, and understanding his revelation. There is a mutuality in knowing. The sheep know the shepherd's voice, just as he knows them. In verse 14 we read 'I know my own, and my own know me.' 'Following' suggests the following of a disciple in faith.

v.5 'Stranger' is one of the designations of the enemy. Not only will the sheep not follow the stranger, but they will 'flee' ('run' in NRSV) from him. Seducers and false teachers may be in mind. Just as there is a union between the shepherd and the sheep, there is a mutual keeping of distance between a stranger and the sheep.

v.6 The term 'figure of speech', in Greek *paroimia*, has two other occurrences in John, at John 16:25 and 29, but the term 'parable', in Greek *parabole,* used frequently in the synoptic gospels, never occurs in this gospel. The Hebrew term underlying both these Greek words is *mashal*, which has different possible senses in English, such as parable, allegory, proverb, simile, and metaphor.

St John Chrysostom comments:
Shepherds always follow behind their sheep, but he, on the contrary, goes before them to show that he would lead all of them to the truth.
(Homilies on the Gospel of John 59.3)

The Good Shepherd by JesusMafa.

How do we describe the sort of discourse we have in John 10? Is it 'a parable with symbolic features', 'a mixture of figurative devices', 'a cryptic discourse'? These have been some of the suggestions from scholars. Even key words like 'door', 'shepherd' and 'fold' are interpreted in a variety of ways in this passage.

In contrast to Mark's Gospel, where the disciples frequently fail to understand Jesus, only occasionally does the Gospel of John, as here, record that the disciples did not understand, literally 'did not know', what Jesus did or said.

v.7 As in verse 1, here too Jesus begins with the words 'Very truly', in Greek *Amen amen*. 'I am the gate for the sheep' is a surprising statement here. In view of the description of shepherding in verses 2-5, we might have expected 'I am the shepherd'. This suggests that different sayings of Jesus have been brought together. One commentator attempted to reconcile the pictures of Jesus as simultaneously shepherd and gate

for the sheep by the idea of the shepherd sleeping across the gateway, thereby acting as a 'human gate'. But such an idea was not in the evangelist's mind.

The gate symbolises that there is only one entrance to the sheep, and one way to the Father, and that is Jesus. The 'gate' statements in verses 7 and 9 are close in meaning to another 'I am' statement of Jesus at 14:6: 'I am the way and the truth and the life. No one comes to the Father except through me.'

v.8 These thieves and bandits 'came before' Jesus and are therefore figures of the past, while the stranger of verse 5, before whom the sheep 'will flee', is apparently a future figure. But the differences of tense do not need to imply that different groups are in mind.

'All who came before me' is rather sweeping. Given the implication that it is by night that thieves and bandits sneak up on the flock, before the shepherd comes through the gate and into the fold in the morning, then the 'thieves and bandits' can hardly be the kings and leaders and prophets of the Old Testament, to whom the sheep did not listen. Probably the Pharisees and other contemporary Jewish teachers are in mind, and perhaps also pagan saviour figures.

v.9 This is a second 'I am the gate' statement, repeating verse 7. There will similarly be two 'I am the good shepherd' statements in verses 11 and 14. 'Gate' may evoke the idea of the gate of salvation, as in the Psalms (e.g. 118:20).

The sheep who enter by Jesus 'will find pasture'. A similar expression is found in Psalm 23:2: 'God makes me lie down in green pastures.' 'Finding pasture' is about the divine life given through Jesus, who gives the bread of life and the water of life to those who come to him.

v.10 'Life' is eternal life, as it always is in John. 'To have life' is fuller and more deliberate than the simple 'to live'. 'To have life abundantly' is having life in its highest degree, which is eternal life.

Matthew 7:13-14 Enter through the narrow gate; for the gate is wide and the road is easy that leads to destruction, and there are many who take it. For the gate is narrow and the road is hard that leads to life, and there are few who find it.

Luke 13:24 Strive to enter through the narrow door; for many, I tell you, will try to enter and will not be able.

These sayings of Jesus in Matthew and Luke are about entering through the narrow gate or door. But while these synoptic sayings speak of entering the Kingdom at the end of time, in John it is Jesus himself who is the means of entry. The focus is on him, rather than the Kingdom. The presentation is more personal, and is not concerned with the end of time but with the present.

The expression 'to have life' is very frequent in John's gospel. Some examples are given below:

3:36 Whoever believes in the Son has eternal life.

5:40 You refuse to come to me to have life.

6:40 This is indeed the will of my Father, that all who see the Son and believe in him may have eternal life.

6:47 Very truly, I tell you, whoever believes has eternal life.

The Good Shepherd

There is of course plenty of Old Testament background for the idea of God as shepherd and God's people as sheep. Ezekiel 34, on the true and false shepherds, is significant: God promises that he himself will be the shepherd of his sheep (verse 15), and that he will send his servant David as their shepherd (verse 23), a statement that may have been interpreted in a messianic sense

v.11 Jesus declares: 'I am the good shepherd.' In various ancient Eastern cultures the reigning monarch was described as 'shepherd'. In the Old Testament the future Messiah king of the house of David was called 'shepherd'.

This shepherd is called 'good', because he lays down his life for his sheep. 'Good' does not mean 'good' as opposed to bad. Since the Greek word used here is *kalos*, usually translated 'beautiful', and not *agathos*, which means 'good', some have translated it as the 'beautiful', or 'noble', or 'model' shepherd. It means much the same as 'true' that is used elsewhere of Jesus: 'the true light' (1:9), 'the true bread' (6:32), 'the true vine' (15:1).

'Lays down his life' is a Hebrew expression, which is not normal Greek usage, and may go back to Jesus' own wording. It is only used in the Johannine writings. It is found four times in this chapter in verses 11, 15, 17 and 18. At 13:37 Peter says to Jesus: 'I will lay down my life for you.' At 15:13 Jesus says: 'No one has greater love than this, to lay down one's life for one's friends.'

In Matthew 7:15, part of the Sermon on the Mount, Jesus says: 'Beware of false prophets, who come to you in sheep's clothing but inwardly are ravenous wolves.'

Addressing the elders from Ephesus in his farewell speech at Miletus St Paul says in Acts 20:29-30: I know that after I have gone, savage wolves will come in among you, not sparing the flock. Some even from your own group will come distorting the truth in order to entice the disciples to follow them.

vv.12-13 The hired hand is contrasted with the good shepherd, who has led his sheep to pasture and proved to be their good shepherd in time of danger. The hired hand is portrayed wholly negatively, typifying those who care nothing for the sheep, and are in the job for selfish reasons. Hired shepherds were in fact common in Palestinian life, and were expected to do everything possible to ward off danger from animals. Unlike the true shepherd, the hired hand has no inner, personal relationship with the sheep. The wolf is the symbol of threatening danger.

vv.14-15 'Knowing' in John's gospel implies care, and it implies love. Relationship is denoted, since in Johannine thought there is mutuality in knowledge and love. The relationship between the Father and the Son is the origin, model and reason for Jesus' communion with his own.

v.16 Jesus has other sheep that do not belong to this 'fold' or 'enclosure'. His flock has members, therefore, in two folds, one Jewish and one Gentile. There will be a merging, or unification, of the sheep of the two folds, so that there will be one flock and one shepherd.

'I must bring them also.' The 'must' suggests that this is God's will. 'They will listen to my voice.' The future tense expresses a strong assurance, which sounds almost like a prophecy. Perhaps even a polemic: any attempt by others to prevent it will be of no avail.

The unity of all believers in Christ, that there will be one flock and one shepherd, is expressed elsewhere in John 11:52. Caiaphas prophesies that the death of Jesus will be 'not for the nation only, but to gather into one the dispersed children of God'. Jesus prays to the Father, at 17:21, 'that they may all be one'. This is an image of the Johannine church, comprised of Jewish and Gentile members.

v.17 Jesus' words here refer to his forthcoming death and resurrection. 'In order to take it up again' implies that the resurrection is more than just what happens after his death. It is the calculated purpose of his laying down his life. His death and resurrection belong inseparably together in Johannine thought.

v.18 The Fourth Gospel portrays the Father and Son acting in unity. In 5:19 we read: 'The Son can do nothing of his own accord, but only what he sees the Father doing.' So there is no contradiction in the thinking in this verse between an action which is commanded by the Father and the same action which is decided by Jesus.

Jesus is here the one who lays down and takes up his life. This contrasts with the frequent statements that 'he was raised' in other New Testament writers. These are two different ways of presenting the reality of the resurrection. The life that Jesus will take up again is not, of course, the same as his incarnate life before the resurrection, but that question is best left to theological enquiry.

Examples of New Testament texts which say that the Father raised Jesus:

Galatians 1:1 Paul an apostle, sent neither by human commission nor from human authorities, but through Jesus Christ and God the Father, who raised him from the dead.

Acts 3:15 You killed the Author of life, whom God raised from the dead.

Acts 4:10 Jesus of Nazareth, whom you crucified, whom God raised from the dead.

Acts 13:30 God raised him from the dead.

The Word Lives On

In the Lectionary

It is on the Fourth Sunday of Easter that this chapter of John's gospel is read. This Sunday has come to be known as 'Good Shepherd Sunday'. In Year A the first ten verses of John 10 are read, the first part of our reading. In Year B the gospel reading begins with the words 'I am the good shepherd' and runs from verse 11 to verse 18, the second part of the text we have been examining. In Year C the verses prescribed are 10:27-30.

The image of the good shepherd is one of the most popular images found in the Gospel of John. It was surely quite natural that the image of the shepherd, used in the Old Testament in texts such as Psalm 23 'The Lord is my shepherd', should have been used also in reference to Jesus. The image is richly explored and elaborated in the Fathers of the Church and in spiritual writers through the centuries.

The Good Shepherd at Catacombs of St. Calixtus, Rome.

Live the Word of God

Listen once more to the reading.

What do you hear now?
Suggestions for reflection and prayer

How can Jesus be compared both to the sheepgate and to the shepherd?

Reflect on the words of Clement of Alexandria given below.

How deeply does the image of the good shepherd speak to you?

The Good Shepherd lays down his life for his sheep.

❖ We pray for those whose lives are at risk due to their Christian faith.

The Good Shepherd has other sheep to bring into the one fold.

❖ We pray for the work of ecumenism and inter-religious dialogue.

The Good Shepherd gives his life freely in order to take it up again.

❖ We pray that faith in the resurrection will inspire all we do.

St Clement of Alexandria, who lived from about 150 until about 215, wrote:

In our sickness we need a Saviour, in our wanderings a guide, in our blindness someone to show us the light, in our thirst the fountain of living water that quenches for ever the thirst of those who drink from it. We dead people need life, we sheep need a shepherd, we children need a teacher, the whole world needs Jesus!

(Christ the Educator 1.9.83)

The Arrest of Jesus

Hear the Word of God

Read John 18:1-12

[1] After Jesus had spoken these words, he went out with his disciples across the Kidron valley to a place where there was a garden, which he and his disciples entered. [2] Now Judas, who betrayed him, also knew the place, because Jesus often met there with his disciples. [3] So Judas brought a detachment of soldiers together with police from the chief priests and the Pharisees, and they came there with lanterns and torches and weapons.

[4] Then Jesus, knowing all that was to happen to him, came forward and asked them, 'For whom are you looking?' [5] They answered, 'Jesus of Nazareth.' Jesus replied, 'I am he.' Judas, who betrayed him, was standing with them. [6] When Jesus said to them 'I am he', they stepped back and fell to the ground.

[7] Again he asked them, 'For whom are you looking?' And they said, 'Jesus of Nazareth.' [8] Jesus answered, 'I told you that I am he. So if you are looking for me, let these men go.' [9] This was to fulfil the word that he had spoken, 'I did not lose a single one of those whom you gave me.'

[10] Then Simon Peter, who had a sword, drew it, struck the high priest's slave, and cut off his right ear. The slave's name was Malchus. [11] Jesus said to Peter, 'Put your sword back into its sheath. Am I not to drink the cup that the Father has given me?'

[12] So the soldiers, their officer, and the Jewish police arrested Jesus and bound him.

Opposite: Book of Hours: Betrayal and Arrest of Christ, Suicide of Judas, Pilate washing his hands.

Understand the Word of God

This session will explore:

❖ the portrayal of Jesus at his arrest

❖ the identity of those who came to arrest Jesus

❖ comparisons with the synoptic gospels

John 20:30 Now Jesus did many other signs in the presence of his disciples, which are not written in this book.

John 21:25 There are many other things that Jesus did; if every one of them were written down, I suppose that the world itself could not contain the books that would be written.

Setting in the Gospel

In this book we are limited to examining twelve texts from the Fourth Gospel. We have had to be selective, even more so than the evangelist (20:30) and the final editor (21:25) of the gospel. As a result, some of the interesting Johannine texts that would require lengthy treatment have had to be left aside, such as the healing of the man born blind (9:1-41), the raising of Lazarus (11:1 -44) and the supper narrative (13:1-30). You are invited to read these while working through this book.

The narrative of the arrest of Jesus follows the long Last Supper Discourse (13:31-16:33) and the prayer of Jesus (17:1-26). After it the Passion Narrative of the Fourth Gospel will continue until the end of chapter 19.

The Taking of Christ. Southern Italy, 11th century.

The Church of All Nations, Gethsemane.

What Kind of Text?

The narrative of the arrest of Jesus establishes important themes that will recur in this Passion Narrative. Jesus is in sovereign control of all that happens to him. His going to a place that Judas knew, as indicated in verse 2, shows that he freely puts himself in danger. In verse 4 we read that he knew 'all that was to happen to him'. When the crowd approaches he goes forward to meet Judas, instead of Judas coming to him and kissing him. He fearlessly declares his identity. He is in control of the situation so that he is taken, but the disciples go free. He shows confident resignation with his words to Peter in verse 11 'Am I not to drink the cup which the Father has given me?'

The Fourth Gospel has no agony in the garden of Gethsemane, although the theme of Jesus' fear and prayer concerning his impending death has been hinted at earlier in 12:27. An agony in the garden would not be appropriate for the Fourth Evangelist. While in the synoptic gospels the narrative of the arrest shows Jesus' greatness, composure and conscious acceptance of suffering, in the Fourth Gospel the arrest reveals his power and majesty.

John 12:27-28 Jesus said: Now my soul is troubled. And what should I say – 'Father, save me from this hour'? No, it is for this reason that I have come to this hour. Father, glorify your name.

Commentary: verse by verse reading

The Arrival of the Crowd

Compare what we read in the Gospel of Mark:

14:26 When they had sung the hymn, they went out to the Mount of Olives.

14:32 They went to a place called Gethsemane; and he said to his disciples, 'Sit here while I pray.'

14:33 He took with him Peter and James and John, and began to be distressed and agitated.

v.1 When the evangelist refers to the words of Jesus this is no doubt a reference back to the discourse and prayer found in John chapters 14-17. The Kidron valley is literally the 'wadi Kidron', a wadi being a rocky watercourse, which is dry except in the rainy season. The Fourth Gospel speaks of the wadi Kidron and a garden. But the two place-names used in the synoptic accounts are not found here: the Mount of Olives, the name of the general area, and Gethsemane ('oil press'), the name of the particular piece of land.

Unlike in the synoptic accounts, Jesus does not detach himself from the main group, and go away with three of them to pray. In what follows in John's account, Jesus will show a special concern for the disciples. While the synoptic accounts emphasised his loneliness, here he is in the garden 'with the disciples'.

It is interesting to compare how the other evangelists narrate the meeting of Judas with Jesus.

Mark 14:45 When Judas came, he went up to Jesus at once and said, 'Rabbi!' and kissed him.

Luke 22:47-48 Judas approached Jesus to kiss him; but Jesus said to him, 'Judas, is it with a kiss that you are betraying the Son of Man?

v.2 Judas is twice referred to as the one 'who betrayed him'. See again in verse 5. The evangelist makes clear to the reader again what Judas was going to do, even though this had been indicated previously during the supper narrative in John 13:21-30.

The evangelist tells us that Jesus often met his disciples in the garden. On this occasion they go to the garden together rather than arranging to meet there. Only John infers that it was Judas' knowledge of Jesus' meeting place with his disciples that enabled him to betray Jesus by taking his captors there. In John, there is no kiss by Judas as a sign of recognition for the captors.

v.3 There are two groups with Judas. The first is a 'detachment of soldiers'. Unlike the other gospels, John appears to be telling us that Roman soldiers were involved in the arrest of Jesus. A detachment is a military term, which could mean a cohort (600 men). It is unlikely there were so many in this case.

The second group is a Jewish one. They are 'police' or 'officers' from the chief priests and the Pharisees. The same two groups will be mentioned again in verse 12. It will be the soldiers, their officer, and the Jewish police who arrest Jesus and bind him.

What are we to make of this involvement, according to John, of Roman soldiers in the arrest of Jesus? Is it historical? Did Pilate place some of his troops at the disposal of the Sanhedrin and the chief priests? Is the arrest of Jesus to be seen as a joint action on the part of the Romans and the Jews?

Many would say that the idea of Roman military participation in the arrest of Jesus is impossible historically. For one reason, according to John's narrative, in verse 13 Jesus is taken to the former high priest, Annas. Since it was the Romans who had deposed Annas from his life-long office as high priest in favour of Caiaphas, it is difficult to see Roman soldiers taking Jesus to him. Probably what we are being given is more of a theological representation than a factual report. The evangelist wishes to show in the arrest of Jesus, just as in his trial before Pilate and his crucifixion, the participation of both Jews and Gentiles, the whole unbelieving world.

The Jewish officers or 'police' are said to have come from 'the chief priests and the Pharisees'. Mark 14:43 states that the crowd that came out to arrest Jesus came from the chief priests and scribes and elders. John is the only evangelist to speak of the Pharisees' involvement in the arrest.

They came with lanterns and torches and weapons. The synoptic gospels simply say that those who came upon Jesus were armed with swords and clubs (*Mark* 14:43). John's lanterns and torches are part of the symbolism of the scene. It had been said that 'it was night' when Judas departed from the supper in John 13:30. The arrest of Jesus is a scene of darkness. There is irony in their coming with man-made objects that give so little light to apprehend the one who is the light of the world.

Annas, the father-in-law of Caiaphas, was high priest from 6 to 15 AD. Despite being deposed he continued to hold an influential position in the Sanhedrin, the governing body of the Jews. He was succeeded as high priest by his five sons and his son-in-law, Joseph Caiaphas, who was high priest from 18 to 36 AD. According to John 11:50 it was Caiaphas who said to the members of the Sanhedrin that it would be better for one man to die for the people than to have the whole nation destroyed. It appears that Caiaphas was prepared to dispose of Jesus in order to avoid any reprisals from the Romans.

Jesus Addresses the Crowd

v.4 Jesus' knowledge of what was happening to him recalls John 13:1, where it was stated that Jesus 'knew that his hour had come to depart from this world and go to the Father'. Jesus takes the initiative and approaches them. This is one reason why the kiss of betrayal by Judas would be out of place in this account.

v.5 'Jesus of Nazareth' is literally 'Jesus the Nazarene'. This is the same title that Pilate will place on the cross, together with the words 'the king of the Jews' (19:19). Jesus identifies himself saying 'I am he.' As we shall see again in verse 6, the evangelist also intends this as a reference to the name of God. This statement by Jesus has the central place in the narrative. Jesus is not handed over powerless, but surrenders himself, thereby showing his power and majesty. The passion story begins only because Jesus allows it to begin.

Judas is described as 'standing with them', hinting at his standing alongside the enemies of Jesus. This is the final appearance of Judas in this gospel.

v.6 Falling down before God's majesty is a well-known biblical theme. Here, however, it is the enemies of Jesus who fall down when Jesus says 'I am.' The reaction of the Roman soldiers and Jewish officers signifies their confusion, helplessness, and powerlessness before the might of God.

It seems unlikely that rough Roman soldiers, with little or no knowledge of Israelite religion, would fall to the ground on hearing a Jewish man they had never seen before say 'I am.' Taken literally, the text is problematic. The evangelist is demonstrating that Jesus went to his passion in a free and dignified manner, with his true identity shown when his enemies recoil and fall to the ground. We might say that the symbolism is correct, but the history is forced.

vv.7-8 Even in his arrest, he shows himself to be the shepherd of those who belong to him, caring for them, so that no harm should come to them, and retaining his superiority and composure, just as in his trial before Pilate he will not surrender to physical force or threats.

Jesus' response to those who come to arrest him in John is quite different from its equivalent in the synoptic gospels. In Mark 14:48-49 he says to them: 'Have you come out with swords and clubs to arrest me, as though I were a bandit? Day after day I was with you in the temple teaching, and you did not arrest me.'

Fr Marie-Joseph Lagrange was a French Dominican biblical scholar who founded the Biblical School (Ecole Biblique) in Jerusalem in 1890. In his commentary on this section of the Gospel of John Fr Lagrange has this to say:
In saying these words Jesus placed in his tone and in his look something of the divine power which resided in him. This is a clear indication, and the only one, that everything he will suffer he will tolerate freely, not being conquered by the prince of this world

v.9 It is not often that the fourth evangelist writes about the fulfilment of something that Jesus has said. In 18:32 there is another instance of this. More usually fulfilment refers to something in the Old Testament.

This saying of Jesus about not losing anyone has not in fact occurred in the Fourth Gospel in precisely this form. But in John 10:28 Jesus states that no one would snatch the sheep from the good shepherd. This background is clearly significant here. In ensuring that the disciples are free to go, Jesus is acting as the good shepherd, who is willing to lay down his life for his sheep (*John* 10:11). For this reason John, unlike Mark and Matthew, does not narrate a flight of the disciples when Jesus is arrested. The reference by these two evangelists to the text of Zechariah 13:7 (in *Mark* 14:27 and *Matthew* 26:31), 'I will strike the shepherd and the sheep will be scattered', would not fit with John's Jesus, who is the shepherd of the sheep even in his passion.

Fulfilment in the Passion Narrative of John:

18:32 This was to fulfil what Jesus had said when he indicated the kind of death he was to die.

19:24 This was to fulfil what the scripture says, 'They divided my clothes among themselves, and for my clothing they cast lots.'

19:36 These things occurred so that the scripture might be fulfilled, 'None of his bones shall be broken.'

The Kidron Valley in Winter.

Mark 14:47 But one of those who stood near drew his sword and struck the slave of the high priest, cutting off his ear.

Matthew 26:51 Suddenly, one of those with Jesus put his hand on his sword, drew it, and struck the slave of the high priest, cutting off his ear.

Luke 22:49-51 When those who were around him saw what was coming...... Then one of them struck the slave of the high priest and cut off his right ear. But Jesus said, "No more of this!" And he touched his ear and healed him.

The image of the cup in the Jewish scriptures:

Habakkuk 2:16 The cup in the Lord's right hand will come around to you, and shame will come upon your glory!

Isaiah 51:17 Stand up, o Jerusalem, you have drunk at the hand of the Lord the cup of his wrath, who have drunk to the dregs the bowl of staggering.

Isaiah 51:22 See, I have taken from your hand the cup of staggering; you shall drink no more from the bowl of my wrath.

Jesus and Simon Peter

v.10 Although all four gospels narrate this incident, only John tells us that the high priest's slave was named Malchus, and that it was Simon Peter who drew his sword. A relative of this high priest's slave will be the third person to accuse Peter of having been in the garden with Jesus at John 18:26. The other gospels are not very clear that it was one of the disciples who cut off the ear of the high priest's slave. Only John and Luke specify that it was the right ear. Only Luke recounts that Jesus heals the man straightaway.

In John, the incident of the ear comes before the seizure of Jesus, while in the synoptic gospels it comes after Jesus is seized, which is perhaps more natural. The fourth evangelist's interest in the incident lies in what Jesus will say in the next verse.

v.11 Jesus speaks of the 'cup' of his death, a metaphor that probably had its origins in the Old Testament idea of the cup of God's wrath. In the synoptic gospels Jesus talks of the cup in the garden of Gethsemane. Jesus says in Mark 14:36: 'Remove this cup from me; yet not what I want, but what you want.'

v.12 The two groups, Roman soldiers and Jewish police, are again mentioned. John is the only evangelist to tell us that they bound Jesus at his arrest. John 18:24 will note that he is sent bound from Annas to Caiaphas.

The Word Lives On

In the Lectionary

These twelve verses at the beginning of John 18 are of course the opening verses of the Passion according to John, which is solemnly read or chanted during the afternoon Liturgy of Good Friday. This reading covers the whole of John 18 and 19. This is the only time that this text is prescribed in the lectionary. The reading of the Passion is preceded by a reading of the Fourth Song of the Servant (*Isaiah* 52:13-53:12), the chanting of Psalm 31 (30), with the refrain 'Into your hands I commend my spirit' and a reading from the Letter to the Hebrews (*Hebrews* 4:14-16 and 5:7-9). A brief homily may be given after the reading of the Passion, and the Service continues with the General Intercessions, the Veneration of the Cross, and Holy Communion.

From the Catechism of the Catholic Church:

The desire to embrace his Father's plan of redeeming love inspired Jesus' whole life, for his redemptive passion was the very reason for his Incarnation. And so he asked, 'Shall I not drink the cup which the Father has given me?'

(paragraph 607)

The Taking of Christ by Michelangelo Caravaggio, (1571-1610).

Live the Word of God

A recent document of the Pontifical Biblical Commission states:

The Gospels reveal that the fulfilment of God's plan necessarily brought with it a confrontation with evil, which must be eradicated from the human heart. This confrontation puts Jesus at odds with the leaders of his people, just like the ancient prophets. Already in the Old Testament, the people of God were seen under two contrasting aspects: on the one hand, as a people called to be perfectly united to God, and, on the other, as a sinful people. These two aspects could not fail to manifest themselves during Jesus' ministry. During the Passion, the negative aspect seemed to prevail, even among the Twelve. But the resurrection showed that, in reality, the love of God was victorious and obtained for all the pardon of sin and a new life. (The Jewish People and their Sacred Scriptures in the Christian Bible 78)

Listen once more to the reading.

What do you hear now?

Suggestions for reflection and prayer

What strikes you about this evangelist's portrayal of Jesus in the garden?

Reflect on the words from the Pontifical Biblical Commission given in the margin.

How strong is Jesus' concern for others as his arrest proceeds?

Jesus demonstrates his sublime freedom in the events of his arrest.

❖ Pray for an understanding of what freedom really is.

Jesus faces the violence of the crowd coming to apprehend him.

❖ Pray for the courage to face violence without fear.

Jesus is aware that the Father's will is being fulfilled.

❖ Pray for an acceptance that God may allow us to travel forward on paths that are hard and painful.

The Garden of Gethsemane by John Millar Watt.

The Death of Jesus

Hear the Word of God

Read John 19:28-37

28 After this, when Jesus knew that all was now finished, he said in order to fulfil the scripture, 'I am thirsty.' 29 A jar full of sour wine was standing there. So they put a sponge full of the wine on a branch of hyssop and held it to his mouth. 30 When Jesus had received the wine, he said, 'It is finished.' Then he bowed his head, and gave up his spirit.

31 Since it was the day of Preparation, the Jews did not want the bodies left on the cross during the sabbath, especially because that sabbath was a day of great solemnity. So they asked Pilate to have the legs of the crucified men broken and the bodies removed. 32 Then the soldiers came and broke the legs of the first and of the other who had been crucified with him. 33 But when they came to Jesus and saw that he was already dead, they did not break his legs. 34 Instead, one of the soldiers pierced his side with a spear, and at once blood and water came out. 35 He who saw this has testified, so that you also may believe. His testimony is true, and he knows that he tells the truth.

36 These things occurred so that the scripture might be fulfilled, 'None of his bones shall be broken.' 37 And again another passage of scripture says, 'They will look on the one whom they have pierced.'

Understand the Word of God

This session will explore:

- ❖ the final words of Jesus on the cross
- ❖ the manner of his death
- ❖ the events following the death of Jesus

Setting in the Gospel

This passage occurs immediately after Jesus' words to his mother and the disciple whom he loved in verses 25-27. Preceding that came the dividing of his clothes by the soldiers and the casting of lots for his tunic in verses 23-25.

It is followed by the account of the burial of the body of Jesus by Joseph of Arimathea and Nicodemus in verses 38-42, which brings the Passion Narrative in the Fourth Gospel to its end.

Christ on the Cross, the Holy Women and St. John the Evangelist, from the Altarpiece of the Parlement de Paris by French School, (15th century).

What Kind of Text?

This may look like straightforward narrative, but it contains some significant theological symbolism. Jesus is the paschal lamb who is slain. Not one bone of his is broken. From his pierced body flow blood and water.

While there have been no Old Testament quotations in John's narrative of the arrest and trial of Jesus, a cluster of Old Testament allusions occurs now, at the crucifixion.

In John 19:24, concerning the dividing of Jesus' clothes and the casting of lots, there has already been a quotation from Psalm 22:18 'They divide my clothes among themselves, and for my clothing they cast lots.'

The cluster of Old Testament quotations in verses 28 and 36-37 directs the reader towards understanding the crucifixion as the revelation and fulfilment of God's purpose in history. For the evangelist, it was perhaps part of his demonstration to the Jews that Jesus as the promised Messiah fulfilled the promises of Scripture.

Crosier Head depicting the Paschal Lamb.

Commentary: verse by verse reading

The final words of Jesus and his death

v.28 Jesus knew 'that all was now finished'. This emphasises the importance of the things that have preceded: the casting of lots for his clothing and seamless tunic, and Jesus' words to his mother and the disciple.

We are unable to specify what scripture is fulfilled when Jesus cries out 'I am thirsty.' It could be a reference to Psalm 69:21, 'for my thirst they gave me vinegar to drink'. It should be noted, however, that Psalm 69:21 refers to a hostile action, while the action which follows Jesus' cry here is evidently an act of kindness.

There is great irony in the fact that Jesus, the source of living water (*John* 7:38), cries out in thirst. He had said that his food was to do the will of the one who sent him, and complete his work (*John* 4:34), and before his arrest Jesus had said, 'Am I not to drink the cup that the Father has given me?' (*John* 18:11). 'I am thirsty' may therefore have the fuller meaning that he thirsts to drink to the last drop the cup he has been given, and thereby accomplish the Father's will.

Mark 15:23 And they offered him wine mixed with myrrh; but he did not take it.

Mark 15:36 And someone ran, filled a sponge with sour wine, put it on a stick, and gave it to him to drink, saying, 'Wait, let us see whether Elijah will come to take him down.'

v.29 The gospels narrate two instances of Jesus being offered a drink during the Passion Narrative. Mark (15:23), and also Matthew but not John, describe a first offering of drink to Jesus, which takes place before he is crucified. Jesus refuses this drink of wine mixed with myrrh, which was intended to dull his senses.

The second incident, recorded here in John, is also found in Mark (15:36) and Matthew but with a different setting and meaning. In the version in Mark and Matthew, if the action is done in kindness, the words that accompany it are said in mockery.

In John's version, by contrast, this is the response when Jesus cries out 'I am thirsty.' There are no words of mockery, so that it appears to be a humane and kind action. In verse 30 Jesus drinks the sour wine. It is presumed that it was the soldiers who offered the drink to Jesus. 'Sour wine' is given as 'vinegar' in some translations. It was a diluted, vinegary drink, often consumed by soldiers and labourers.

While in Mark and Matthew it is offered 'on a stick' (probably a long, strong stalk), in John it is offered 'on a branch of hyssop'. Hyssop is a shrub related to mint and thyme. Its branches would be suitable for sprinkling, but the stem would hardly bear the weight of a soaked sponge. In the book of Exodus hyssop is used to sprinkle the blood of the paschal lamb on the doorposts of the Israelites. Its occurrence here recalls the Passover, in a narrative in which Jesus was sentenced by Pilate at the very hour (noon) when the Passover lambs were slaughtered in the temple (*John* 19:14). Another Passover allusion will be found in verse 36.

Exodus 12:21-23 Then Moses called all the elders of Israel and said to them, 'Go, select lambs for your families, and slaughter the Passover lamb. Take a bunch of hyssop, dip it in the blood that is in the basin, and touch the lintel and the two doorposts with the blood in the basin. None of you shall go outside the door of your house until morning. For the Lord will pass through to strike down the Egyptians; when he sees the blood on the lintel and on the two doorposts, the Lord will pass over that door and will not allow the destroyer to enter your houses to strike you down.'

Hyssop plant.

v.30 Jesus' final words in the Fourth Gospel, 'It is finished', imply that he has done all that the Father gave him to do. In the Fourth Gospel the final words of Jesus indicate that he is in control. After saying those last words 'he bowed his head and gave up the spirit', the two verbs of action perhaps implying that he chose the moment of his death in bowing his head. At John 10:17-18 the good shepherd had said, 'No one takes my life from me, but I lay it down of my own accord. I have power to lay it down, and I have power to take it up again.'

The final words of Jesus in the other gospels are as follows:

Mark 15:34 Jesus cried out with a loud voice, 'Eloi, Eloi, lema sabachthani?' which means, 'My God, my God, why have you forsaken me?'

Luke 23:46 Then Jesus, crying with a loud voice, said, 'Father, into your hands I commend my spirit.'

Matthew 27:46 is similar to Mark's text.

The Events after the Death of Jesus

v.31 The Day of Preparation usually referred to the day before sabbath when all those things allowed on the sabbath, such as cooking, chopping wood, drawing water, and travelling, were done. This was the period from daytime until the evening on the Friday, when the sabbath began. The statement 'that sabbath was a day of great solemnity' refers to John's understanding that, in the year of Jesus' death, the Passover fell on a sabbath.

For John, unlike for the synoptic evangelists, Jesus is going to be buried towards the end of Passover Preparation day (on a Friday afternoon), which will be followed by the Passover which is also a sabbath day, beginning on the Friday evening. This means that for John, Jesus has not died on Passover Day itself, and his supper with his disciples on the previous evening cannot have been a Passover meal.

The synoptic evangelists present a different explanation: the supper was indeed a Passover meal and Jesus dies on Passover Day. Some argue that John's presentation is more plausible.

Deuteronomy 21:22-23 When someone is convicted of a crime punishable by death and is executed, and you hang him on a tree, his corpse must not remain all night upon the tree; you shall bury him that same day.

The Jews did not want bodies left on the cross 'during the sabbath'. The wording might give the impression that it was because of the approach of sabbath that they wanted the bodies removed. Sabbath would have given an added impetus to what they wanted, but the Jewish practice was that the bodies of those crucified should be buried before sunset on whatever day. Normal Roman practice in other places was to leave the bodies of the crucified on the cross as a warning to would-be criminals.

The breaking of the legs was usually done with a heavy mallet. While in itself a cruel action, it was a mercy towards those crucified, since it hastened their death. Evidently the Jews think that Jesus must still be alive when they make their request to Pilate.

vv.32-33 Pilate agrees to the request of the Jews.

v.34 While the synoptic evangelists record the words of the centurion at Jesus' death, in John a quite different action of a Roman soldier is reported. 'Pierced his side' means something like 'stabbed at' or 'prodded' his side with a spear. This is a kind of exploratory jabbing to verify whether the victim was in fact dead. Jesus' side will be mentioned in the resurrection appearances later in the gospel (*John* 20:20, 25, and 27).

There has been a great deal of writing about the significance, both medically and symbolically, of the flow of blood and water from the side of Jesus. Some thought that the incident was narrated because it was thought to be a miracle. But as the miraculous aspect is not underlined by the evangelist this would not seem to be its purpose. There is a theological meaning and symbolism here.

A dead body does not usually bleed once the heart has stopped pumping, although a flow of blood is possible from a wound received very soon after death, and John's narrative, with the Jews expecting Jesus to be still living, would suggest a recent death. The water could be lymph, a colourless, bodily fluid. The difficulty is its apparent sharp separation from the blood. Doctors have speculated about the possible medical explanations for the phenomenon that is reported.

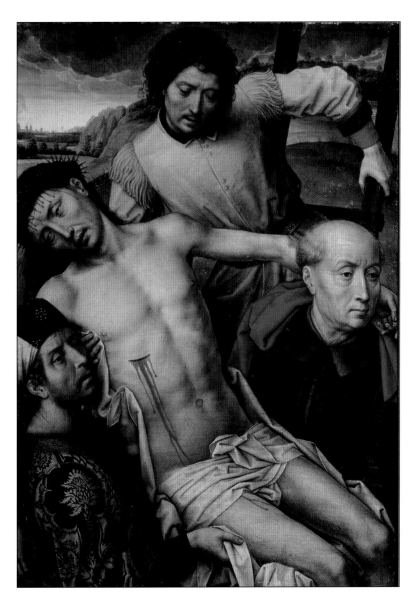

Descent from the Cross, left hand panel from the Deposition Diptych, c.1492-94 by Hans Memling, (c.1433-94)

v.35 Evidently this matter is of importance to the evangelist, for he insists on the truthfulness of the testimony. Unless the writer is referring to himself in the third person ('he who saw it', rather than 'I'), the writer of these words appears to be someone different from the one who communicated the information. The one who communicated the information could of course be the disciple whom Jesus loved, since he was present at the cross before the death of Jesus (19:26).

Descent from the cross by Harmenszoon van Rijn Rembrandt.

One clear meaning of the incident is that Jesus truly died on the cross, and that his resurrection was not the revival from coma of someone who had not really died. Some think that this point was directed against the Docetists, heretics who asserted that the humanity of Jesus and his crucifixion were not real, but were an illusion.

Water is something life-giving in the Fourth Gospel. In 7:37-38 Jesus says: 'Let the one who believes in me drink. As the scripture has said, Out of his heart shall flow rivers of living water.' The Fathers interpreted this in the sense that the Spirit would flow abundantly from the heart of Christ. Blood also is life-giving in the Fourth Gospel, with almost all the references in John 6:53-56, the eucharistic section of the Bread of Life discourse.

We can therefore take as a primary meaning of this incident the association of life-giving properties with the dead body of Jesus. Once his sacrifice is complete the flow of life for the world begins.

v.36 'None of his bones shall be broken' seems to be a reference to the instructions about the eating of the paschal lamb at Passover. In Exodus 12:46 we read: 'The Passover shall be eaten in one house; you shall not take any of the animal outside the house, and you shall not break any of its bones.' The theme of Jesus as the paschal lamb reaches back to the beginning of this gospel and to John the Baptist's testimony: 'Behold the lamb of God who takes away the sin of the world.' (1:29)

v.37 The quotation in this verse is taken from Zechariah 12:10. The original Hebrew text is difficult to understand. 'They shall look upon me, whom they have pierced. And they shall mourn for him as for an only child, and weep for him as for a first-born.' John's version of the text is somewhat different.

In the way that John uses it, who are 'they'? It seems to have a general meaning. Other texts about Jesus being 'lifted up' might help our understanding.

1 John 5:6-8 appears to make the same point, about the reality of the death of Jesus, when it states that Jesus 'is the one who came not with the water only, but with the water and the blood'. It asserts the reality of the life and work of Jesus, from his baptism in water, to the blood he shed on the cross, the two demarcations of his work on earth.

'Blood' and 'water' also have a sacramental significance in the Fourth Gospel. Blood as we have seen in 6:53-56, and water in the words to Nicodemus, about being begotten of water and Spirit in 3:5. This raises the question of whether the evangelist intends a sacramental reference here.

John 3:14-15 Just as Moses lifted up the serpent in the wilderness, so must the Son of Man be lifted up, that whoever believes in him may have eternal life.

John 8:28 When you have lifted up the Son of Man, then you will realise that I am he.

John 12:32 And I, when I am lifted up from the earth, will draw all people to myself.

The Word Lives On

In the Lectionary

These verses from John 19 are part of the reading of the Passion according to John, which is solemnly read or chanted during the afternoon Liturgy of Good Friday. The whole of chapters 18 and 19 is read.

John 19: 31-37 are read on the Solemnity of the Sacred Heart of Jesus in Year B. The preface for this feast uses the same imagery: 'From his wounded side flowed blood and water, the fountain of sacramental life in the Church. To his open heart the Saviour invites all men, to draw water in joy from the springs of salvation.'

Christ on Cross with Donors and Saints c1450-1516.

Live the Word of God

Listen once more to the reading

What do you hear now?

Suggestions for reflection and prayer

What are the special features of John's story of the death of Jesus?

Reflect on the words from the Catechism of the Catholic Church given in the margin.

How important for this evangelist is the idea that the Scriptures must be fulfilled?

The evangelist displays a deep appreciation of the Scriptures of Judaism.

❖ Pray for a greater understanding of the Jewish roots of our Christian faith.

The evangelist shows Jesus facing death with patience and equanimity.

❖ Pray for constancy amid all the trials of life.

The evangelist assures us of the truth of this testimony.

❖ Pray that more people may perceive and embrace the truth of the gospel.

From the Catechism of the Catholic Church:

In his Passover Christ opened to all the fountain of Baptism. He had already spoken of his Passion, which he was about to suffer in Jerusalem, as a 'Baptism' with which he had to be baptised. The blood and water that flowed from the pierced side of the crucified Jesus are types of Baptism and the Eucharist, the sacraments of new life. From then on, it is possible 'to be born of water and the Spirit' in order to enter the Kingdom of God.

(paragraph 1225)

The Appearances of
Jesus to the Disciples

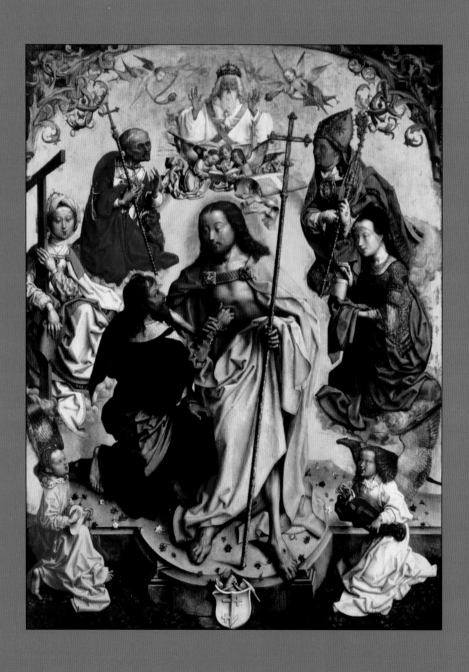

Hear the Word of God

Read John 20:19-29

[19] When it was evening on that day, the first day of the week, and the doors of the house where the disciples had met were locked for fear of the Jews, Jesus came and stood among them and said, 'Peace be with you.' [20] After he said this, he showed them his hands and his side. Then the disciples rejoiced when they saw the Lord. [21] Jesus said to them again, 'Peace be with you. As the Father has sent me, so I send you.' [22] When he had said this, he breathed on them and said to them, 'Receive the Holy Spirit. [23] If you forgive the sins of any, they are forgiven them. If you retain the sins of any, they are retained.'

[24] But Thomas, who was called the Twin, one of the twelve, was not with them when Jesus came. [25] So the other disciples told him, 'We have seen the Lord.' But he said to them, 'Unless I see the mark of the nails in his hands, and put my finger in the mark of the nails, and my hand in his side, I will not believe.'

[26] A week later his disciples were again in the house, and Thomas was with them. Although the doors were shut, Jesus came and stood among them, and said, 'Peace be with you.' [27] Then he said to Thomas, 'Put your finger here and see my hands. Reach out your hand and put it in my side. Do not doubt, but believe.' [28] Thomas answered him, 'My Lord and my God!' [29] Jesus said to him, 'Have you believed because you have seen me? Blessed are those who have not seen and yet have come to believe.'

Opposite: Doubting Thomas placing his hand into Christ's wound, c.1499, Master of the altarpiece of St. Bartholomew (c.1485-1510).

Understand the Word of God

The Gospel of John has two conclusions, which are informative about the intention and the process of writing:

20:30-31 Now Jesus did many other signs in the presence of his disciples, which are not written in this book. But these are written so that you may come to believe that Jesus is the Messiah, the Son of God, and that through believing you may have life in his name.

21:25 But there are also many other things that Jesus did; if every one of them were written down, I suppose that the world itself could not contain the books that would be written.

This session will explore:

❖ the appearances of the risen Jesus

❖ peace and forgiveness

❖ the profession of faith of Thomas

Setting in the Gospel

Taking place on the day of the resurrection, the first appearance of Jesus to the disciples follows the discovery of the empty tomb by Peter and the disciple whom Jesus loved (*John* 20: 1-10), and Mary Magdalen's recognition of the risen Jesus (*John* 20: 11-18). Jesus sent her to tell the brothers with the words, 'I am ascending to my Father and your Father, to my God and your God.'

After our passage, in verses 30-31, comes the conclusion of the gospel. John chapter 21 is considered an appendix and is probably by another writer.

Noli Me Tangere, 1442 by Fra Angelico.

What Kind of Text?

The gospel accounts of the appearances of the risen Jesus to the disciples are quite varied. Mark has a summary of the appearances of the risen Jesus in the additional verses at the end of chapter 16 (16:9-20). Matthew 28:16-20 narrates an appearance on a mountain in Galilee. Luke 24:36-50 has the closest similarities to the Gospel of John in that the appearance of Jesus takes place in Jerusalem on Easter night, and in verses 47-49 the themes of forgiveness of sin, witnessing, and the Spirit occur. John's account seems to be independent of Luke's, as well as of the other synoptic gospels.

View from inside Tomb

Commentary: verse by verse reading

The first appearance of Jesus to the Disciples

v.19 The disciples are presumably the Twelve minus Judas. John never calls them apostles, and rarely calls them the Twelve.

We have no indication as to where they were staying. Acts 1:13 has them in an upper room after the Ascension, and some identify that upper room with the room where the last supper took place. That might be wishful thinking, and it is not part of the evangelist's concern.

The risen Jesus is not impeded by locked doors, which were locked for fear of the Jews. With the leader of the movement now killed, one might have thought that the disciples would have little to fear from the Jews, which presumably means the religious authorities. But they could have had cause for fear of being accused of stealing the body of Jesus, and putting round disturbing stories of his resurrection. Fear of the Jews was mentioned previously in relation to Joseph of Arimathea, who was a secret disciple (*John* 19:38).

The Hebrew word for peace shalom is still used as a greeting today. It corresponds to the Arabic greeting salam. The concept of shalom is very rich. It refers not only to the absence of war and hostility, but to all that fosters the well-being of the individual and community. Although the gospel is written in Greek and uses the Greek word for peace eirene, the idea found here retains the richness of the Hebrew shalom and has a new fulness which is the result of the new life of the risen Lord and all that this implies for his disciples.

Jesus stood among them and said, 'Peace be with you.' While this is a known Jewish greeting, it has in this context the meaning of the overcoming of fear and confusion, and it becomes in a special way an Easter greeting, as the repetition in verse 21 suggests. In Luke 24:36 also the risen Jesus says to the disciples: 'Peace be with you.'

v.20 Jesus shows them his wounds in order to demonstrate that it is he. Luke 24:40 too speaks of his showing them his hands and feet: 'And when he had said this, he showed them his hands and his feet.'

In John they 'rejoiced when they saw the Lord'. In Luke 24:37 they were 'startled and terrified, and thought that they were seeing a ghost'.

v.21 This is the commissioning of the disciples. The verb 'send' is used some forty-three times in the Fourth Gospel of the Father sending Jesus. Now it is used of Jesus sending out his disciples. The Father's sending of the Son still continues, but the Son gives the disciples a share in that sending, for the continuation of his work on earth. Once again Jesus brings peace.

v.22 The Church is now equipped for her mission, by the giving of the Holy Spirit. This is John's equivalent of the Pentecost Narrative in Acts chapter 2. Some would say that it is better put across here, in that Jesus is the agent of the sending down of the Holy Spirit, while in the account in Acts Jesus is absent, having physically departed ten days previously.

'He breathed on them' may hint that this is the act of new creation. The same verb was used in the Greek version of Genesis 2:7: 'God breathed on his face the breath of life, and the man became a living being.'

'Receive the Holy Spirit' could be translated as 'receive holy spirit', in that there is in the Greek no definite article before 'spirit' and no differentiation of capital letters. Obviously what the Fourth Evangelist reports Jesus as saying may not yet have the precision of the Church's subsequent understanding of the personhood of the Holy Spirit.

Jesus Appears to the Disciples Gathered Under One Roof for Fear of the Jews by the Italian School, (15th century).

In the book of Ezekiel the two actions of giving the spirit and forgiving sin are connected:

Ezekiel 36:25-26 I will sprinkle clean water upon you, and you shall be clean from all your uncleannesses, and from all your idols I will cleanse you. A new heart I will give you, and a new spirit I will put within you.

Many Catholics imagine that this saying is about the sacrament of Penance, perhaps forgetting that frequent and repeated private confession was not known before the 7th century, and that baptism is the primary forgiveness of sins for the Christian. We profess in the Creed: 'We believe in one baptism for the forgiveness of sins.'

v.23 'Forgive' and 'retain' are literally 'release' and 'hold fast'. 'They are forgiven' is known as a 'divine passive': it is God who does the forgiving. Jesus entrusts to his Church, not only his mission from the Father, but also his power over sin - to isolate, repel and cancel it. The power to forgive sin appears to be closely connected with the giving of the Spirit in verse 22, without restricting the work of the Spirit to just the forgiving of sin.

The expression 'to forgive sin' has never previously occurred in the Fourth Gospel, though at the beginning John the Baptist had described Jesus as 'the lamb who takes away the sin of the world' and 'the one who baptises with the Holy Spirit' (*John* 1:29 and 33). John 20:23 has 'forgive' before 'retain', emphasising the primacy of salvation. It is a saying about the Church's and the disciples' mission.

The Upper Room: traditionally held to be the place of Jesus' appearance to the disciples.

The Second Appearance of Jesus to the Disciples

v.24 In verses 19-23 there was no hint that Thomas was not present with the other disciples so that it comes as a surprise to the reader to learn that he was not there. Nor was there any mention of doubt or hesitation on the part of the disciples.

In verses 24-29 Thomas carries or personifies the doubt or questioning of the whole group, making the disciples appear less culpable as a group. It will occur to the reader that, had Thomas been present when Jesus unexpectedly appeared, then he too would have believed. Thomas' previous appearances in this gospel suggest that he is slow to understand the Lord's way (14:5), but nevertheless loyal to Jesus (11:16).

Despite Jesus' words to him in 20:27, literally 'do not be unbelieving', and the frequency with which people speak of 'doubting Thomas', he is a type, not of the unbeliever as such, but of the person who is weak in faith. Belief in its fulness will come to him only as the gift of the risen Lord.

Although verse 24 describes Thomas as 'one of the twelve', there were actually only eleven of them now, and 'the twelve' is used rarely in the Fourth Gospel (*John* 6:67, 70, 71). It probably occurs here because it was used in the oral, catechetical version of this story before the gospel was written down.

v.25 A brash assertion is made by Thomas. This is the only mention of 'nails' in any of the gospels, and they are mentioned only in relation to the hands of Jesus, not his feet. Thomas' words 'unless I put my hand in his side' presuppose John 19:34 and the soldier piercing the side of Jesus with a spear, and they suggest a wound of considerable size.

Other gospel accounts of the appearances of the risen Jesus mention the doubts and hesitations of the disciples:

Matthew 28:17 When they saw him, they worshipped him; but some doubted.

Luke 24:11 But these words seemed to them an idle tale, and they did not believe them.

Luke 24:37-38 They were startled and terrified, and thought that they were seeing a ghost. He said to them, 'Why are you frightened, and why do doubts arise in your hearts?'

v.26 The fact of the disciples still being in Jerusalem a week after the resurrection seems to conflict with the tradition in Mark 16:7 and Matthew 28:7 and 16 that Jesus directed them to meet him in Galilee. In John 21, added by another Johannine writer, Jesus does meet them in Galilee.

'A week later' is literally 'eight days later'. The Christian celebration of Sunday as opposed to the Jewish sabbath may already have been established by the time that this was written, and at its Sunday observance the Johannine church probably reminded itself of the Lord's appearance to Thomas and the other disciples.

v.27 The fact of Jesus knowing and being able to repeat what Thomas had said to his fellow disciples in verse 25 seems to impress Thomas in his questioning. 'Do not doubt, but believe' is literally 'do not be unbelieving, but believing'.

Did Thomas actually probe with his finger and hand, as invited to by Jesus? The point is not of interest to the evangelist, who is more interested in the change that occurs in Thomas' attitude.

Interesting questions arise, again not of interest to the narrator, concerning the glorified resurrection body of Jesus: that it could pass through closed doors and yet retain some physicality in appearance, with nail marks in the wrists, and a hole in the side.

v.28 We note the personal tone of the repeated 'my'. Thomas has found his Lord and his God, in the Risen One whom he now recognises. During the ministry of Jesus 'Lord' (in Greek *kyrios*) had only been used as an address (as in *John* 6:68 and 11:12). Now it is used as a profession of faith. 'God' is added, leaving no doubt about the faith that Thomas has found.

This double acclamation by Thomas is the climax of this narrative, and of the gospel. At the end of the gospel, Thomas' confession corresponds to the statement at the beginning of the Prologue 'and the Word was God' (*John* 1:1). Some commentators have suggested that 'my Lord and my God' reflects a challenge to the emperor cult, specifically that promoted by Domitian, emperor from 81-96 AD, who styled himself as 'our Lord and God' (*Dominus et deus noster*).

v.29 While our translation from the New Revised Standard Version gives Jesus' words as a question, 'Have you believed because you have seen me?', a number of other translations give it as a statement. The Jerusalem Bible reads: 'You believe because you can see me.' There is of course no punctuation in the Greek manuscripts. There is no great difference in meaning, whichever translation is chosen. Thomas' faith is not being doubted. It is the how of his faith that is being commented on.

It might seem unfair that the disciple whom Jesus loved was implicitly praised by the evangelist for seeing and then believing: at the empty tomb, with the cloth and the linen wrappings lying there 'he saw and he believed' (20:8). But in Thomas' case, when his fellow-disciples gave witness concerning the Lord's resurrection, his stubbornness and his reliance on seeing meant that he was remaining in the past and in failure.

'Blessed are those who have not seen and yet have come to believe.' This is a beatitude and it recalls what Jesus had said during his ministry, as recorded in the synoptic gospels, 'Blessed are the eyes that see what you see.' (*Luke* 10:23 *Matthew* 13:16). The disciples no longer see him with their eyes, or hear him with their ears. The era of signs in his ministry and of appearances after his resurrection has passed. But the post-apostolic era is not inferior to the ministry of Jesus. This is an important truth for the readers of the Gospel.

Thomas' confession is the climax to a whole series of confessions of Jesus throughout this gospel:

1:49 Nathanael: Rabbi, you are the Son of God! You are the king of Israel!

4:42 The Samaritan woman: We know that this is truly the Saviour of the world.

6:69 Peter: We have come to believe and know that you are the Holy One of God.

9:35-37 Jesus asks: 'Do you believe in the Son of Man?' The man who was born blind replies: 'Lord, I believe.'

16:30 The disciples: Now we know that you know all things. We believe that you came from God.

20:16 Mary Magdalen: Rabbouni.

1 Peter 1:8 expresses a similar outlook: Although you have not seen him, you love him; and even though you do not see him now, you believe in him and rejoice with an indescribable and glorious joy.

Opposite: The Incredulity of St. Thomas, 1602-03 by Michelangelo Merisi da Caravaggio, (1571-1610).

Jesus Appears to the Disciples Together Under One Roof by Italian School.

The Word Lives On

In the Lectionary

It is not surprising, given that the second appearance of Jesus in this narrative takes place 'on the eighth day', one week after the resurrection, that this text is read on the Second Sunday of Easter, also known as Low Sunday. The gospel reading laid down to be read that day also includes the two verses which follow our passage, verses which form the conclusion of the gospel, before the appendix in chapter 21.

It should also not surprise us that the account of the first appearance of Jesus, from verse 19 to verse 23, with the Easter gift of the Spirit on the disciples by Jesus, is the gospel reading for the Mass on Pentecost Sunday.

Finally, the feast of St Thomas the Apostle, celebrated on 3rd July, has John 20:24-29 as the gospel reading at Mass.

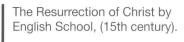
The Resurrection of Christ by English School, (15th century).

Live the Word of God

Listen once more to the reading.

What do you hear now?

Suggestions for reflection and prayer

What for you is the basis of faith, seeing or believing?

Reflect on the words from the Catechism of the Catholic Church given on the next page.

The chair of St.Peter, detail of the stained glass window behind, 1665 by Giovanni Lorenzo Bernini, (1598-1680).

Do you believe it is unfair to refer to Thomas as 'doubting Thomas'?

The Risen Jesus brings his peace to the disciples.

❖ Pray for openness to receive the gifts of peace and forgiveness.

The Risen Jesus brings the Holy Spirit.

❖ Pray for a renewal of the gifts received at Confirmation.

The Risen Jesus invites faith which goes beyond what can be seen.

❖ Pray for faith and trust in the testimony of the gospel.

Above: The Dove of the Holy Spirit, 1360-70 by Giusto di Giovanni de' Menabuoi, (d.1393).

In its section on the Sacrament of Confirmation the Catechism of the Catholic Church states:

This fulness of the Spirit was not to remain uniquely the Messiah's, but was to be communicated to the whole messianic people. On several occasions Christ promised this outpouring of the Spirit, a promise which he fulfilled first on Easter Sunday and then more strikingly at Pentecost. Filled with the Holy Spirit the apostles began to proclaim 'the mighty works of God', and Peter declared this outpouring of the Spirit to be the sign of the messianic age. Those who believed in the apostolic preaching and were baptised received the gift of the Holy Spirit in their turn. (paragraph 1287)

The Prologue

Hear the Word of God

Read John 1:1-18

[1] In the beginning was the Word, and the Word was with God, and the Word was God. [2] He was in the beginning with God. [3] All things came into being through him, and without him not one thing came into being. What has come into being [4] in him was life, and the life was the light of all people. [5] The light shines in the darkness, and the darkness did not overcome it.

[6] There was a man sent from God, whose name was John. [7] He came as a witness to testify to the light, so that all might believe through him. [8] He himself was not the light, but he came to testify to the light. [9] The true light, which enlightens everyone, was coming into the world.

[10] He was in the world, and the world came into being through him; yet the world did not know him. [11] He came to what was his own, and his own people did not accept him. [12] But to all who received him, who believed in his name, he gave power to become children of God, [13] who were born, not of blood or of the will of the flesh or of the will of man, but of God.

[14] And the Word became flesh, and lived among us, and we have seen his glory, the glory as of a father's only son, full of grace and truth. [15] John testified to him and cried out, 'This is he of whom I said, 'He who comes after me ranks ahead of me, because he was before me." [16] From his fulness we have all received, grace upon grace. [17] The law indeed was given through Moses; grace and truth came through Jesus Christ. [18] No one has ever seen God. It is God the only Son, who is close to the Father's heart, who has made him known.

Saint Jean l'Evangeliste by El Greco, (1541-1614) 17th century.

Understand the Word of God

This session will explore:
- ❖ the coming of the Word
- ❖ the reception given to the Word
- ❖ the effects of this coming

Saint John the Baptist by Titian (1477/89-1576).

Setting in the Gospel

The opening of the Fourth Gospel, which was possibly added to it at a second stage of editing, the early Christian hymn that we call 'the Prologue', is a magnificent and exalted introduction and an excellent summary of the thought and theology of the gospel. This is a good reason for looking at it last rather than first in our study of the Fourth Gospel.

The Prologue precedes the first narrative section of the Fourth Gospel, which speaks of the witness of John the Baptist.

What Kind of Text?

The Prologue is a hymn to Jesus as Logos, the Word, which celebrates his existence both before and after taking on human flesh. It makes no mention of the resurrection and exaltation of Christ, so that some have wondered whether Christ's victory might have been mentioned in a verse which has not been preserved. In regard to subject-matter, it is a hymn not about God as such, but about God in relationship to humanity.

One issue concerns where reference to the incarnation occurs. It is certainly present in verse 14: 'The Word became flesh and lived among us.' But we can detect it possibly also in verses 5, 10 and 11, which highlight the acceptance or rejection of the light.

The Prologue displays significant literary and theological differences from the rest of the gospel. It displays a 'staircase' or 'climactic' parallelism, in which it keeps going back on the last word or expression used.

Such parallelism can be seen in verses 3-5: without him not one thing came into being. What has come into being in him was life, and the life was the light of all people. The light shines in the darkness, and the darkness did not overcome it.

The Prologue contains words and expressions that occur nowhere else in the gospel, such as 'Word', 'fulness', and 'grace and truth'. This is the reason why some think that the Fourth Evangelist is not the author of this hymn. Otherwise, why do such important terms never occur again in the gospel? A few of them, such as 'grace' (Greek *charis*) and 'fulness' (Greek *pleroma*), are used by St Paul.

The main theme, the pre-existence and the incarnation of the Logos, is found or reflected in the rest of the gospel in a very limited way.

Possible references to pre-existence in the rest of the gospel:

1:30 (John the Baptist says) This is he of whom I said, 'After me comes a man who ranks ahead of me because he was before me.'

8:58 (Jesus says) Very truly, I tell you, before Abraham was, I am.

17:5 (Jesus says) So now, Father, glorify me in your own presence with the glory that I had in your presence before the world existed.

Commentary: verse by verse reading

The Word

In the third clause, 'the Word was God', in the Greek original text, the definite article 'the' is not used before 'God', as might be expected in Greek. But if the intention was simply to say that the Word was 'divine', the adjective for 'divine' (theios), could have been used. The absence of 'the' does not imply that the Word was less than God, or not quite God, but rather suggests that there was not a complete personal identification between God and the Word, and that there was some differentiation or distinctness between them.

v.1 The phrase 'in the beginning' appears deliberately chosen to echo Genesis 1:1, which begins 'In the beginning God created the heavens and the earth.' Light, darkness and life, about which we will hear later, are also Genesis themes. Creation itself is mentioned in verse 3.

The Greek word *Logos* (= Word) appears three times in this first verse, and again in verse 14. These are the only occurrences in the whole of the Fourth Gospel.

The Wisdom books of the Old Testament, such as Proverbs and the book of Wisdom, used lofty, metaphorical descriptions of the wisdom which was related to God. The book of Wisdom described wisdom as 'a breath of the power of God, a pure emanation of the glory of the Almighty, a reflection of eternal light' (*Wisdom* 8:25-26). In the Prologue these metaphors are left behind and divine being is attributed directly to the Word.

v.2 This verse repeats what was said in verse 1. Such repetitions are characteristic of the Prologue and are known as 'staircase parallelism'.

The Gnostics spoke of a Demiurge (a Greek word meaning 'craftsman'), an inferior deity responsible for the creation of material things, which were imperfect and in opposition to God. The teaching of the Gnostics was strenuously opposed by early Church fathers, such as St Irenaeus, who stressed the importance of fidelity to the tradition.

v.3 This verse concerns creation. The Word is stated to have been the agent of creation, even though it is expressed repetitiously: 'all things came into being through him, and without him not one thing came into being'. There is no doubt that the Logos, who according to verse 1 is united most intimately to God, is God's active collaborator in creation.

'What has come into being in him was life.' Is this natural life or eternal life? Many think it to be the second, because 'life' in the Johannine writings always means eternal life, and the next clause identifies that life as 'the light of all people'. The statement that 'without him not one thing came into being' may possibly be an attack on the Gnostics, who considered that the material world came from an inferior deity. In this case, in defending the universal role in creation of the Logos, the

Prologue would indirectly be defending the goodness of all created things.

v.4 The focus is the relationship of the Logos to the world of humanity. Just as he was the giver of existence to all creation, so for humans he is the vehicle of everything that gives fulness to their existence. 'Life' is the more basic idea, perhaps, and 'light' a specification of it. Compare the saying of Jesus at 8:12: 'Whoever follows me will have the light of life.'

v.5 Light and darkness are frequently mentioned in the Fourth Gospel. Darkness obviously means the world estranged from God, to which human beings yield.

The idea of the light overcoming darkness has more than one meaning. It can mean 'overcome' or 'quench', on the one hand, or 'grasp' or 'understand', on the other. The darkness has neither quenched the light nor understood the light. If 'understand' is the primary meaning, it prepares for statements in verse 10 and verse 11 that people did not know or accept the light. The present tense 'shines' is used deliberately: the Logos illuminates unceasingly.

Jesus speaks of light and darkness in these words to Nicodemus:

3:19-21 And this is the judgement, that the light has come into the world, and people loved darkness rather than light because their deeds were evil. For all who do evil hate the light and do not come to the light, so that their deeds may not be exposed. But those who do what is true come to the light, so that it may be clearly seen that their deeds have been done in God.

The Northern Lights.

John sent by God

vv.6-7 'There was a man sent by God.' 'Sent' in the Fourth Gospel usually refers to Jesus, as the one sent by the Father, but in this instance it is used of John the Baptist, whose mission was also from God.

'He came as a witness to testify to the light.' He testifies to Jesus, the light of the world (*John* 8:12 and 9:5). 'Witness' and 'testify' are both related to the Greek *martyria*, which means 'witness', and are frequently used terms in the gospel. Witness or testimony is given in order that others may believe.

v.8 When it is stated that John the Baptist was not the light, this may be directed against a sect who followed John the Baptist, claiming that he was the light, and that he was superior to Jesus because he came before him in time. At 5:35 Jesus himself describes John the Baptist as a lamp: 'He was a burning and shining lamp, and you were willing to rejoice for a while in his light.'

Sunrise.

v.9 'The true light, which enlightens everyone, was coming into the world.' This translation is preferable to another possible translation: 'He was the true light that enlightens everyone coming into the world.'

He is the 'true' light not just in contrast with worthless, false lights, but as expressing the fulness of being and reality of God. How the light comes is not stated until verse 14. He comes in an unforeseen manner, by becoming flesh.

The Reception of the Word

v.10 This seems to refer to Jesus the Word, although some prefer to understand these verses of God's Word in Old Testament times.

v.11 This is similar to the statement in verse 10 about the world not knowing him. 'What was his own' and 'his own people' are different forms of the same Greek word, *idios*. Elsewhere in this gospel, the word *idios* is used in a different, stricter sense of those in union with Jesus. In John 13:1 we read 'He loved his own who were in the world.'

v.12 'Who believed in his name' is actually a present tense, 'who believe in his name'. The 'name' is his name as God. Believing 'in his name' is an expression used only by John.

Those who receive him become children, not sons and daughters. The word 'son' is reserved for Jesus. In the New Testament childhood of God is a gift, not a natural quality that people are born with. In the Sermon on the Mount we read: 'Blessed are the peacemakers, for they will be called children of God.' (*Matthew* 5:9) This stresses the power conferred by God. Humans cannot of themselves attain to being children of God.

v.13 These words are added by the evangelist to explain the supernatural origin of the children of God. This is not birth in a natural way. This seems to allude to Christian baptism.

The Jerusalem Bible, following some Latin manuscripts, has a singular reading, which apparently refers to the virginal conception of Jesus. It reads: 'who believe in the name of him who was born not of blood or of the will of the flesh or of the will of man, but of God.' This reading is found only in some Latin manuscripts, and in no ancient Greek manuscript. It is therefore most unlikely to be the original reading.

Other examples of believing 'in his name'

John 2:23 When he was in Jerusalem during the Passover festival, many believed in his name because they saw the signs that he was doing.

John 3:18 (Jesus said) Those who believe in him are not condemned; but those who do not believe are condemned already, because they have not believed in the name of the only Son of God.

1 John 3:23 And this is his commandment, that we should believe in the name of his Son Jesus Christ and love one another, just as he has commanded us.

1 John 5:13 I write these things to you who believe in the name of the Son of God, so that you may know that you have eternal life.

Recall what Jesus said to Nicodemus:

John 3:3 'Very truly, I tell you, no one can see the kingdom of God without being born from above.'

John 3:5 'Very truly, I tell you, no one can enter the kingdom of God without being born of water and Spirit.'

Grace and truth

v.14 This is the first use of the term Logos, 'Word', since the first verse of the chapter. In the Prologue the incarnation has been presupposed at least since verse 9, or even verse 5, but is only now made explicit.

'The Word became flesh' is an aorist, point in time, past tense. The Latin Creed has: '*Et incarnatus est.*' This suggests a change in the mode of being of the Logos. Before, he was in glory with the Father. Now, he takes on the lowliness of human, earthly existence. In Greek thought, any idea of the Logos becoming flesh would have been preposterous. The Logos was viewed as the principle of cosmic order. It could not possibly become bound to flesh.

The verb 'to dwell' used in the Greek, skenoun, seems to have been deliberately chosen to resemble in sound the Hebrew verb shakan, which means rest, abide or dwell. This word is used to describe God's dwelling among the people of Israel, as in Exodus 25:8: Have them make me a sanctuary, so that I may dwell among them.

'Lived' or 'dwelt' among us uses the Greek verb *skenoun* which is related to *skene*, meaning 'tent'. The Word pitched his tent among us. This recalls the statement about wisdom in the book of Ecclesiasticus, also called Sirach: 'The Creator of all things gave me a command, and my Creator chose the place for my tent. He said: Make your dwelling in Jacob, and in Israel receive your inheritance.' (24:8) This presence among humanity of the Word surpasses whatever was said of wisdom in earlier Jewish writings.

'Glory' is the term used of the Word becoming flesh. It is God's glory that is meant. The ministry of Jesus manifests this glory from the beginning. After the wedding at Cana the evangelist wrote: 'He revealed his glory.' (*John* 2:11)

In the fourth century, the biblical term monogenes was employed against the Arian claim that the Son was made or created, and given the sense of 'only begotten'. This corresponds to the Latin term unigenitus. Against the claims of the Arians, the Creed had to assert that the Son is 'begotten, not made' (in Latin genitum non factum).

The designation 'only son' is used in the New Testament only in the Fourth Gospel and in the First Letter of John. It will occur again at verse 18. The Greek word *monogenes* means 'of one kind', 'only' in the sense of 'unique', 'special', 'specially loved', and it alludes to Abraham and his specially loved son, Isaac. Isaac was Abraham's special son and his heir, but he was not Abraham's only son. There was also Ishmael.

The pair of nouns 'grace and truth' (in Greek *charis* and *aletheia*) sound very much like the Old Testament pair of terms *hesed* and *emeth*, which mean 'steadfast love' and 'faithfulness'. These two nouns are used in reference to the giving of the covenant at Exodus 34:6, and in many other places, including the Psalms.

'Grace' is not one of John's terms. In its usage here, it would refer to both the riches of grace of the Word, and the gift that humans receive from him. 'Truth' in this usage does not have its Johannine sense of God's truth as revealed in Jesus, but probably keeps its Old Testament sense of 'faithfulness' and 'fidelity'.

v.15 This verse sounds like an intrusion into the text of the Prologue. Verse 14, ending 'full of grace and truth', would lead much more smoothly into verse 16: 'From his fulness we have all received, grace upon grace.'

v.16 This is the joyful confession of all who have received Christ in faith, not just the apostolic generation, but even believers of a later date who did not see him during his life on earth.

'Grace upon grace'. The Greek preposition *anti*, here translated as 'upon', does not recur in the gospel, so that we are not precisely sure of the sense intended. The idea could be that of the accumulation of ceaseless streams of grace succeeding one another.

v.17 The contrast of the law given through Moses and grace and truth coming from Jesus Christ might sound much more like St Paul than St John. It is somewhat rhetorical, and should not be read as stating the absence of all grace and truth in the law given through Moses.

Portrait of Saint John. Book of Kells, 6th century manuscript of the Four Gospels.

v.18 That no-one has seen God is stated in other places in the Gospel. John 6:46 reads: 'Not that anyone has seen the Father except the one who is from God. He has seen the Father.' Moses, unlike 'the only Son', has not seen God face to face. Hence the old dispensation could not convey 'grace and truth' in its fulness.

'God the only Son' is the best attested reading. The text appears to say that only God can reveal God. 'Only' is the same word *monogenes* as in verse 14, with its background in the Abraham and Isaac story.

'Who is close to the Father's heart', literally 'in the bosom of the Father', is a metaphorical way of saying 'with God', as in verse 1. God the only Son has made God known. All that we can know about God the Father we have learnt through Jesus.

Ten Commandments written on stone tablets in Hebrew.

Alpha and Omega.

The Christmas hymn 'Of the Father's love begotten' is a rendering of a poem on the incarnation by Aurelius Prudentius, who died in the fifth century.

Of the Father's love begotten
Ere the worlds began to be,
He is Alpha and Omega,
He the Source, the Ending He,
Of all things that are and have been,
And that future years shall see:
Evermore and evermore.

Blessed was the day for ever
When the Virgin, full of grace,
By the Holy Ghost conceiving,
Bore the Saviour of our race,
And the child, the world's Redeemer,
First revealed his sacred face:
Evermore and evermore

The word lives on

In the lectionary

Given its exalted presentation of the incarnation, it is not surprising that John 1:1-18 is read at the Mass of the Day on Christmas Day. It is also read on 31st December, and is laid down in the lectionary as the gospel for the second Sunday after Christmas, provided no other feast takes the place of the Sunday.

It is of interest also to note that the Prologue was regularly read for many centuries at the end of Mass. This custom dates from the thirteenth century and the reading of John 1:1-14 was laid down in the Missal of Pope Pius V issued in the wake of the Council of Trent. It became known as the 'last gospel'. It was removed from the celebration of Mass in 1964 in order to allow the structure of the Mass, the Liturgy of the Word and the Liturgy of the Eucharist, to be seen more clearly.

That this is a particularly venerated gospel reading is now recalled by its repeated use at the heart of the celebration of Christmas.

Live the Word of God

St John Chrysostom writes:

By no means did the Lord diminish his own nature by his condescension, but he raised us, who had always sat in disgrace and darkness, to unspeakable glory. Likewise, it may be that a king, conversing with interest and kindness with a poor person of lower social status, does not shame himself at all but makes the other illustrious and observed by all.

(Homilies on the Gospel of John 11.1)

Listen once more to the reading.

What do you hear now?
Suggestions for reflection and prayer

What does the Prologue of John's gospel mean to you?

Reflect on the words of St John Chrysostom given in the margin.

What do these verses tell us about God's attitude to humanity?

Grave Marker for St. John the Apostle at Selcuk near Ephesus.

The Word was with God and was God.

❖ Pray for a deeper appreciation of God's mystery.

The Word was a light shining in the darkness.

❖ Pray that we may bring the light of Christ into the darkness of people's lives.

The Word pitched his tent among us.

❖ Pray in gratitude for God's becoming one of us.

Introductory page to the Gospel of St. Matthew depicting winged symbols of the Four Evangelists framed in panels, from the Book of Kells, c.800.

Picture Credits

Cover   Celtic manuscript depicting St. John the Evangelist, ©Photos.com

P.9   St. John the Baptist, 1513-16, Leonardo da Vinci, (1452-1519) / ©Ashmolean Museum, University of Oxford, UK/ The Bridgeman Art Library Nationality / copyright status: Italian / out of copyright

P.11   Bodmer P75 manuscript

P.12   Stained Glass in Modern Catholic Church. ©Stock.Xchng.

P.14   Elijah in the Desert, Washington Allston, (1779-1843) / Museum of Fine Arts, Boston, Massachusetts, USA / The Bridgeman Art Library.

P.17   ©Pascal Deloche/Godong/Corbis.

P.18   White dove in her flight. ©Stock.Xchng.

P.20   From The Adoremus Hymnal, produced by Adoremus: Society for the Renewal of the Sacred Liturgy ©1997, Ignatius Press, San Francisco. Used with permission.

P.21   St. John the Baptist, Jacopo Palma, (Il Vecchio) (c.1480-1528) / ©York Museums Trust (York Art Gallery), UK / The Bridgeman Art Library.

P.22   ©Frank Wesley. www.frankwesleyart.com.

P.24   John the Baptist sees Jesus from Afar, illustration from 'The Life of Our Lord Jesus Christ' James Jacques Joseph Tissot, (1836-1902) / Brooklyn Museum of Art, New York, USA / The Bridgeman Art Library

P.25   Christ with Fishermen, English School, (20th century) / Private Collection / ©Look and Learn / The Bridgeman Art Library.

P.26   The Calling of St. Andrew and St. John, illustration for 'The Life of Christ', c.1886-94, James Jacques Joseph Tissot, (1836-1902) / Brooklyn Museum of Art, New York, USA / The Bridgeman Art Library.

P.29   ©Bibleplaces.com

P31   Fig tree. ©Photos.com

P.33   ©Clipart.com

P.34   ©Clipart.com

P.35   Solid as a rock. ©Stock.Xchng.com

P.36   Wedding at Cana, 2001, Dinah Roe Kendall, (Contemporary Artist) / Private Collection / The Bridgeman Art Library.

P.38   Cretan water jars.

P.39   ©Clipart.com

P.40   ©Clipart.com

P.43   The Marriage at Cana, 1723, Bartolomeo Litterini, (1669-1745) / San Pietro Martire, Murano, Italy / Cameraphoto Arte Venezia / The Bridgeman Art Library.

P.44   The Marriage at Cana, Bohemian School (17th century) / Private Collection / Joanna Booth / The Bridgeman Art Library.

P.45   ©Bibleplaces.com

P.46   ©Photos.com

P.47   The Wedding at Cana. ©Jesusmafa.com

P.48   Christ Talks with Nicodemus, illustration for 'The Life of Christ', c.1886-94, Tissot, James Jacques Joseph (1836-1902) / Brooklyn Museum of Art, New York, USA / The Bridgeman Art Library.

P.50   Nicodemus. ©Jesusmafa.com

P.51   W.107 fol.24r Christ and Nicodemus from the Evangelarium of Santa Giustina written by Laurentius Gazius Cremonensis, 1523-25, Bordone, Benedetto (c.1450-1530) / ? The Trustees of the Chester Beatty Library, Dublin / The Bridgeman Art Library .

P.53   Visit of Nicodemus to Christ, 1880, John La Farge, (1835-1910) Smithsonian American Art Museum, Washington DC, USA. ©Photo Smithsonian American Art Museum/Art Resource/Scala, Florence.

P.57   The Volto Santo, possibly begun by Nicodemus (fl.1150-66), Italian School, (12th century) / Lucca Cathedral, Italy / Alinari / The Bridgeman Art Library.

P.59   W.107 fol.24r Christ and Nicodemus from the Evangelarium of Santa Giustina written by Laurentius Gazius Cremonensis, 1523-25, Bordone, Benedetto (c.1450-1530) / © The Trustees of the Chester Beatty Library, Dublin / The Bridgeman Art Library.

P.60   ©Photos.com

P.61   ©Photos.com

P.62   Christ and the Woman of Samaria, c.1500 (oil on panel) by Juan de Flandes, (c.1465-1519) © Louvre, Paris, France/ Peter Willi/ The Bridgeman Art Library. Nationality / copyright status: Netherlandish / out of copyright.

P.64   Jesus at Jacob's Well, John Millar Watt, (1895-1975) / Private Collection / © Look and Learn / The Bridgeman Art Library.

P.65   Jacob's Well. © PaulsTravelBlog.com

P.67   The Samaritan Woman. ©Jesusmafa.com

P.68   ©Bibleplaces.com

P.70   ©Photos.com

P.72   Christ and the Woman from Samaria at Jacob's Well, section of wing panel from the Mompelgarter Altarpiece, Matthias Gerung or Gerou (c.1500-68/70) / Kunsthistorisches Museum, Vienna, Austria / The Bridgeman Art Library.

P.74   The Feeding of the Five Thousand, Joachim Patenier or Patinir, (1487-1524) / Monasterio de El Escorial, Spain / Giraudon / The Bridgeman Art Library.

P.76   The Feeding of the Five Thousand, 1479,by Alexander Bening, British Library, London.©Photo Scala Florence/HIP.

P.77   ©Photos.com

P.122   ©Photos.com

P.124   Christ on the Cross, the Holy Women and St. John the Evangelist, from the Altarpiece of the Parlement de Paris, French School, (15th century) / Louvre, Paris, France / Giraudon / The Bridgeman Art Library.

P.125   Crosier Head depicting the Paschal Lamb, possibly 12th century with more recent mounts, / ©Ashmolean Museum, University of Oxford, UK / The Bridgeman Art Library.

P.127   Hyssop, Hyssopus officinalis. ©age fotostock / SuperStock

P.129   Descent from the Cross, left hand panel from the Deposition Diptych, c.1492-94, Hans Memling, (c.1433-94) / Capilla Real, Granada, Spain / Giraudon / The Bridgeman Art Library.

P.130   ©Photos.com

P.132   ©Photos.com

P.134   ©Photos.com

P.136   Noli Me Tangere, 1442, Angelico, Fra (Guido di Pietro) (c.1387-1455) / Museo di San Marco dell'Angelico, Florence, Italy / The Bridgeman Art Library.

P.137   ©Bibleplaces.com

P.139   Fol.135v Jesus Appears to the Disciples Gathered Under One Roof for fear of the Jews, Italian School, (15th century) / Biblioteca Reale, Turin, Italy / Alinari / The Bridgeman Art Library.

P.140   ©Bibleplaces.com

P.142   The Incredulity of St. Thomas, 1602-03, Caravaggio, Michelangelo Merisi da (1571-1610) / Schloss Sanssouci, Potsdam, Brandenburg, Germany / Alinari / The Bridgeman Art Library.

P.144   Fol.137r Jesus Appears to the Disciples Together Under One Roof, Italian School, (15th century) / Biblioteca Reale, Turin, Italy / Alinari / The Bridgeman Art Library.

P.145   The Resurrection of Christ, English School, (15th century) / Ferens Art Gallery, Hull City Museums and Art Galleries / The Bridgeman Art Library.

P.146   The chair of St.Peter, detail of the stained glass window behind, 1665, Bernini, Giovanni Lorenzo (1598-1680) / St. Peter's, Vatican, Rome, Italy / The Bridgeman Art Library.

P.147   The Dove of the Holy Spirit, 1360-70, Giusto di Giovanni de'Menabuoi, (d.1393) / Padua Baptistery, Padua, Italy / Alinari / The Bridgeman Art Library.

P.148   Saint Jean l'Evangeliste, 17th cent, El Greco, (1541-1614) Prado, Madrid. © White Images/Scala, Florence.

P.150   Saint John the Baptist, Titian (1477/89-1576) Accademia, Venice. © Photo Scala, Florence - courtesy of the Ministero Beni e Att. Culturali.

P.153   ©Photos.com

P.154   Texas Gulf Coast-Seabrook. ©Stock.Xchng.

P.157   ©Photos.com

P.158   Ten Commandments written on stone tablets in Hebrew. ©Stockxpert.

P.159   Alpha and Omega.

P.160   Grave Marker for St. John the Apostle. © Kristi J. Black/Corbis.

P.161   MS 58 fol.27v Introductory page to the Gospel of St. Matthew depicting winged symbols of the Four Evangelists framed in panels, from the Book of Kells, c.800, Irish School, (9th century) / © The Board of Trinity College, Dublin, Ireland / The Bridgeman Art Library.

Notes